CREWS for CRUISE

Fifth Edition

The Publishers extend grateful thanks to the many Cruise Lines & Personnel Executives who gave their time, help and advice towards the furtherance of this publication.

"CREWS FOR CRUISE"
The Official Cruise Ship Job Guide
Fifth Edition
Compiled, researched & written by
John Kenning
Published by
Harp Publications Ltd
Thames House Swan Street Old Isleworth Middlesex TW7 6RJ

First published 1990 by Harp Publications
New edition reprinted 1991 by Harp Publications
Revised and reprinted 1992 by Harp Publications
Completely revised & reprinted 1994 by Harp Publications Ltd
Revised and reprinted 1995 by Harp Publications Ltd

Copyright 1995 John Kenning & Harp Publications Ltd
A catalogue record for this book is available from the British Library

ISBN: 1 898308 05 5

Cover design and layout:
ADDA. Thames House Swan Street Old Isleworth TW7 6RJ
Edited by: Suzanne Juta
Printed by: Aaron Printing Ltd., East Molesey, Surrey

CONTENTS

Page:

A MESSAGE FROM JOHN KENNING ....

Congratulations! And thank you for ordering this book. You have just taken your very first step towards an exciting and well paid new career - living and working on board one of the many luxury cruise ships that sail all around the world.

First, let me tell you a little about how I decided to embark upon a career at sea, and also about this book.

My name is John Kenning. It's several years now since I obtained my first job on a cruise ship (I was a ship's photographer incidentally.) In my work, I sailed all over the world, meeting many interesting, beautiful and very wealthy people. I also met many members of the opposite sex who would sometimes visit me in my darkroom and help me 'develop' a closer relationship with them - you should see my collection of holiday snaps! I literally lived a life of luxury, and got paid for it too! Above all, life was fun and uncomplicated. I was visiting many foreign lands at an age when most of my friends were still living with their parents. I was enjoying the company of charming young ladies, while my friends were lucky if they got a date with the spotty girl next door. It certainly wasn't because I was better looking, or any different than any of my friends but I did, and still do, have an adventurous spirit; I love meeting people and having fun. I needed excitement in my life and I wanted to travel and earn some sensible money too.

Of course, when I first had the idea of working on a cruise ship, it wasn't easy. In fact, I really didn't have a clue where to start and how to go about it; you see, I didn't have a copy of this book then! But through sheer persistence and determination, I succeeded in gaining employment with several cruise lines. And I must instill in you now, that determination is something you're going to need yourself, if you wish to achieve your objective.

So, after spending several years cruising, I came to the conclusion, that if I could do this - so too, could other people ... yes YOU. And that's how "Crews for Cruise" (or ˙C4C' as I call it) was born. Initially, I set about compiling the book from personal experience and from current research; that was back in 1990. However, you are now reading the fifth edition and I have to say that it is certainly a vast improvement on the earlier volumes. This has been mainly due to the many cruise ship lines and personnel managers who gave valuable help and assistance in the compilation of this, the very latest ˙Crews for Cruise' - The Official Cruise Ship Job Guide.

In this book I'm going to tell you how to find those sought after jobs, and how to apply so that you stand the very best chance of success. Plus I'll reveal a few little (sometimes slightly 'sneaky') tips and 'tricks of the trade' that should help you gain an edge over the other people who are also trying to find out about the vacancies on offer! Simply follow the instructions I give you, and very shortly - with a bit of hard work and maybe also a little bit of luck - you could be steaming off to the Mediterranean, the Caribbean, the South Pacific, or some of the many other exciting destinations on offer!

Now, I don't claim that 'Crews for Cruise' is the only guide you'll find. But it is **the very best!** 'Crews for Cruise' is the **only** FULL LENGTH HANDBOOK and the only guide that really tells you everything you need to know, written by someone who has actually worked on a cruise ship. I don't just give you a list of addresses and tell you to get on with it. I tell you EXACTLY what to do to stand the best chance of success. And the Directory of Employers contained in this book is the longest, most detailed and most up to date that I know of.

'Crews for Cruise' has been so successful that, as I've already mentioned, it is now in its fourth edition. My publishers are even selling copies to cruise ship crews who are using it to look for their NEXT jobs. So if you'll excuse a little immodesty, I really do think 'Crews for Cruise' is Number One .... If you're going to get a job at all, you're going to get it using the information contained in this book!

So now, if you're ready .... let's get on with the guide. I'd advise that you read it through thoroughly first. Maybe twice if possible. Don't be too hasty to make your first application. When you fully understand how things work, and what you must do, then you can start applying for the jobs.

Your first job could be just a few weeks away!

I wish you every success and Bon Voyage,

John Kenning.

PS. I'm always delighted to receive letters from readers telling me about the jobs they obtain. So, once you've arrived on your ship and settled in, please do write and tell me who you're working for, what you're doing, and how you're getting on! Your advice and tips will then be featured in the next edition of 'Crews for Cruise'.

LIFE ON BOARD

OK, I hear you say, but what is life on board really like? A fair question! You may have heard about cruise ships or liners - call them what you will - being like floating hotels ... floating palaces some might say. Certainly, the more luxurious liners are palatial on a scale you simply cannot imagine. Their sheer size is unbelievable. Just try to visualise a tower block of flats turned on its side with a funnel on top. Even then it might be dwarfed by some cruise ships! You will live and eat well, perhaps too well - you'll need to watch your waistline! Crew's quarters are clean and comfortable although not luxurious. Your cabin may be situated closer to the engine room than those of the passengers (and as you travel free, I suppose this is only fair). The noise from the engines can be annoying at first, but don't worry, you'll soon get used to it.

Before we go any further, it is worth remembering a very important point. The passengers on board cruise ships are all VIP's - they should be (and indeed expect to be) pampered and powdered. After all, they are indirectly going to be paying your wages. Also, if you give good service, you'll probably be rewarded not just in monetary terms but also in job satisfaction too. And you might even get a marriage proposal ... it really does happen and I should know!

There is NOTHING quite like life on board a cruise ship. It's exciting. It's fun. You'll never dread getting up for work in the morning and you really can travel the world and get paid for it too! Life is never ever boring and fellow crew members are usually easy-going, friendly and of course, the passengers are on holiday and in a happy mood. The atmosphere on board is relaxed and bubbly. Depending on the job you choose, you'll probably be able to mingle with the passengers and join in much of the fun. I was able to participate in the dances and functions and even eat at the Captain's table occasionally.

Once you have successfully gained employment, I'm not going to kid you that life on board is one long holiday. Work can be hard, hectic and sometimes downright frantic. I've worked all hours of the day and sometimes all night getting orders ready for passengers before they leave the ship the following day. And depending on your position on board, you may be required to work seven days a week. However, when you do reach port, almost everyone enjoys a rest period and you'll be able to go ashore and explore foreign, and often exotic places. Obviously, depending on the line you've shipped with, this can be a few hours, days or even weeks.

In port, try to go ashore with other crew members at first, as they will know the best places to visit. A word of warning; some foreign docklands can be dangerous areas for single females and even males. However, you will no doubt be warned of such dangers and in these instances, if you wish to go ashore alone, it's best always to take a taxi to and from the ship.

During the time I spent cruising, I made many valuable overseas contacts and friends and whenever I return to foreign lands, I never need to stay in a hotel; old friends always offer me the use of their homes for holidays etc. One thing I'll guarantee, you'll make many friends amongst the passengers and your fellow crew members.

Food on board is excellent and plentiful; alcoholic drinks are charged at duty-free prices. Many recreational facilities are provided solely for the crew and these can include mess room, library, video room, gymnasium, swimming pool, shop etc. If you're fortunate enough to sail to sunny climes, remember to pack your camera, swimming togs and suntan lotion. However, there is always a shop on board and you'll usually qualify for staff discounts on many necessities and luxuries. Cigarettes, perfumes and bottles of booze are all available at duty-free prices; and you may even get discounts on these items too. So living aboard a cruise ship is cheap and if you want to save, this is an excellent opportunity to do so. And don't forget, your salary will almost certainly be tax-free too.

Cabin and deck parties abound. Virtually every night someone will throw a party - more about these affairs later in the book!

Most cruise ships are superbly stabilised nowadays, to ensure maximum comfort for passengers and crew. If you do suffer from seasickness, you may feel uncomfortable for the first two or three days on your initial voyage. This will pass as you get used to the ship's motion - this is known as getting your 'sea legs'.

Each cruise ship carries literally hundreds of crew members (I'll tell you more about this later on in the book). Crews are constantly changing and new ships are being introduced by companies eager to cash in on the cruise ship boom. There are always openings and there are always vacancies. It's a flamboyant lifestyle ... are you ready for it?!

Upon acceptance of your job application, you'll be asked to enter into a contract which is fair to both parties, for the duration of the voyage. If the voyage terminates at a different location from your embarkation point, you'll usually either be flown back, or you may be asked to enter into a new contract on a return ship. However, the majority of cruises are 'round trips' - in other words, you sail to a number of destinations and return to the same point, the duration of which can be a matter of just days, weeks, or even months, depending on the distance travelled.

During my life on board, I always found cruise companies to be honest and caring towards the crew. Let's face it, if they were to rip crew members off, they just wouldn't last a minute, so don't be afraid to tread boldly. But by all means obtain legal advice before signing a contract if you wish. However, I'd be very surprised if your contract isn't completely fair to both you and them. After you arrive back home, and providing your employer was happy with you, no doubt you'll be asked to return for another trip ... but more about that later.

Safety on Board
Since this book was first published, I have received a few letters regarding the safety of cruise ships. To say they are 100% safe might be tempting fate; but as far as I know, there has not been a serious peacetime tragedy involving a cruise ship since the *Titanic* went down over eighty years ago - I am not counting the unfortunate *Estonia* disaster, as this was a car ferry and not an ocean-going liner in the true sense. But please don't worry about hitting huge icebergs and sinking; it just doesn't happen these days! Occasionally, you may hit a thick sea mist or fog. This isn't dangerous either thanks to the sophisticated radar technology that all ships carry. I have worked on ships in some of the roughest seas imaginable - believe me, if there was any danger, I would be the first to tell you. I stand to be corrected, but I would imagine that cruise liners probably represent the safest form of transport ever invented - no doubt someone will now write and tell me that rickshaws are 5% safer!

Of course, accidents on board can and do happen. Cruise ships carry a medical team including at least one fully qualified doctor and nurse/s. Should you fall ill, you will receive full medical treatment at no cost. In the unlikely event of serious illness or injury, it has been known for patients to be airlifted to the nearest port. This is, however, extremely rare; nevertheless, you may wish to take out an insurance policy to cover any medical eventuality.

Once on board, you *will* be required to take part in various lifeboat drills - just in case. These are mandatory and, as on board aircraft, certain safety regulations must be legally carried out for the protection of passengers and crew.

Notes:

Chapter 1

WHAT YOU NEED TO KNOW
ABOUT THE CRUISE BUSINESS

The Cruisin' Revolution

Until the 1950's, if you wanted to travel abroad, you had to cruise there; you had no choice. But after the introduction of modern commercial airline travel which obviously sliced days off your trip, gradually the cruise business 'sank', almost without trace. Ships were scrapped, and crews were sacked.

But by the late 1970's, after many years in the doldrums, cruising started to become popular again. This time, however, NOT for transport, but for PLEASURE. Today, cruising is back in fashion with a vengeance!

And the good news is that the cruise lines are now growing rapidly once again. Quite a few of them, including Britain's Cunard and P&O, have bought superb new ships in the last few years. And I know there are many more being built right now; in fact, approximately one new cruise ship is launched somewhere in the world every week!

All these ships, old or new, need CREW. And an awful lot of them too. Would it surprise you to learn that for every ten passengers on a cruise ship there are five crew to look after them?

The Modern Cruise Ship ....
Forget the Titanic !

The modern cruise ship is a wonder in every way, and couldn't be further removed from the old ocean liners which, unless you could afford to travel First Class, often weren't very pleasant at all. It can travel vast distances across the sea, smoothly safely and effortlessly. And it contains every modern comfort you could possibly imagine.

There are luxurious cabins and suites, lavish public rooms, gourmet restaurants, bars, cinemas screening 'first-run' movies, casinos, top nightclubs, health clubs, pools and even tennis courts and gardens! - a place where passengers can spend an amazing few weeks, or just a few days.

Put simply, a cruise ship is a floating HOTEL.

So think of all the jobs that are done in a hotel.

All these - AND MORE - are needed on an average cruise ship!

People are needed to sail the ship. People are needed to maintain it. People are needed to clean it. People are needed to do the office work. People are needed to cook. People are needed to serve the food. People are needed to look after the passengers. People are needed to entertain them. People are needed to do just about anything you can think of!

A cruise ship at sea has to be totally SELF-SUFFICIENT. And because it operates 24 hours a day, several people are needed to do every single job. For example, just one cleaning job needs at least four people, working 40 hours a week each, to carry it through.

So can you see the potential? Chances are that if there is a job for you on dry land there could be a job for you somewhere on one of the cruise ships listed in this book.

Some Facts About Cruise Ships

- The biggest cruise ship in the world is *Majesty of the Seas* owned by Royal Caribbean Cruise Line. At 73,941 tons it carries 2,354 passengers and 827 crew.

- *Queen Elizabeth 2*, owned by Cunard, is, contrary to popular belief, not the largest cruise ship in the world, weighing in at 67,140 tons. But with 1,766 passengers served by almost 1,000 crew is considered the most luxurious.

- Today there are at least 160 other cruise ships in service around the world. It's estimated that over 100,000 people work in the cruise business - I repeat, 100,000!
- An 'average sized' cruise ship, like Royal Caribbean's *Song of Norway*, is 23,000 tons and 630 feet long, carrying 1,000 passengers and 450 crew. Some cruise ships are much larger (as above), others much smaller.

- The main cruise ship nations are Britain, America, Norway, Italy and Greece. There are British ships with Italian waiters, Norwegian ships with British crew, and Greek ships carrying only American passengers!

- The most popular cruising areas are the Caribbean and Mediterranean. Up to 70% of cruise ship passengers are American, and 60% of all cruise ships operate out of Miami and the Caribbean ports.

Coming Down to Earth for a Moment -
Is It Really That Good ?

Of course, it's very easy to get too carried away with dreams of life on the ocean wave. And you might find other cruise ship guides which don't tell you about the drawbacks. Well, I'll set the record straight and come out honestly and say what it is like ....

Absolutely amazing!

In all honesty it really is a great lifestyle. You'll get to travel free, and get paid for it too. Many jobs offer pay, tips, commission and bonuses! Often there is no income tax to pay. Your ship will only take you to the nicest parts of the world - places, like the Caribbean, where if you had to pay to go, you'd be spending up to £2,000 for a short trip!

But it's not all about pay. There's also the way of life, which is wonderful. You get to make great friends, and (if you're lucky) get to know wealthy and famous passengers. There's a great working atmosphere. The social life, on the ship or on the beach, is exciting, free and easy. For many it's the biggest singles' party on earth!

But - The Drawbacks .....
Well, the pay isn't necessarily fantastic (depending on the position you are seeking.) You could perhaps earn more in a similar job on dry land. In some jobs you'll need to depend on tips to make a decent wage.

Don't think you'll be going on a free cruise. Only certain crew members can mix with the passengers and use the ship's luxury facilities. And you won't be cruising in a luxury cabin either! - Crew cabins are usually small, shared and quite basic although they are generally clean and comfortable; after all, most cruise lines adopt the philosophy that a happy ship produces happy passengers - so they strive to keep the crew happy for this reason alone.

Finally, don't expect time off on every tropical island (or even any full days off at all). The working hours can be long and hard. And, when your contract ends (six or eight months is usually the maximum) there's no guarantee you'll be kept on.

In all my time at sea, I loved every minute. I'm sure you will too, but remember it's not all plain sailing!

How to Increase Your Chances
of Finding a Job Twenty Times !

Please remember one thing (and virtually every almost every employer I talk to says the same). Cruise lines generally don't have time to train people to do a job from scratch. So they prefer people who have EXPERIENCE in a similar job on dry land, and who know what to do from day one.

But what if I haven't got any experience?

This needn't be a problem at all. But do aim to get some before you make your first application. For example, you'll remember that I said cruise ships are like floating hotels. So, experience in a hotel and similar places like restaurants, pubs, clubs, leisure centres etc. - anywhere you're serving and looking after the public as guests - is really well worth having.

So why not get a job somewhere like this? Ideally full time, maybe part time. Scan every Job Centre and every newspaper you can find to look for any job that will give you this experience and give it a try!

I know of more than one crew member who have used a very clever technique to get their experience. If there aren't any jobs advertised, then simply call up your local hotels, restaurants, nightclubs etc. Tell them what you're doing. Offer to work part time for FREE. Not many places will refuse such an offer, and it will all be to YOUR BENEFIT. Please believe me, this really does work and although you won't receive any monetary reward immediately, think of it as a long term investment and plan for your future.

Whilst you might just get a cruise ship job without any experience (I did first time, so it does happen) your chances will be so much greater if you can offer some good experience. If need be, go away, get some experience, and come back in a year or so; you'll be rewarded in the long run in. Yes, it may mean waiting a bit longer but it will be well worthwhile if you really want to sail into a job! And I'm sure you'll appreciate my honesty in telling you this - my competitors and imitators are certainly not going to be so honest!

If you want to succeed - take heed! This is very good advice that I'm passing on to you.

Some Other Points
to Consider :

Skills and Qualifications Needed :
Few cruise line employers have any minimum qualification requirements. Very few jobs require specialist qualifications. Mostly, experience is more valuable to you than any certificate.

Sex :
It's almost 50-50 men-women on many ships now. Cruise lines are good equal opportunity employers.

Age :
There are no overall limits. The ideal starting age is 19 - 35.

Marital Status :
Single or married are accepted equally. But it can be stressful for couples who become separated with one spouse at sea. Some lines do employ couples to work together.

Nationality :
There are no restrictions whatsoever. Some cruise lines use low-paid Third World labour for their menial deck jobs. On others, a certain type of work is traditionally undertaken by particular ethnic groups. For example, the Chinese operate the laundry on board many cruise ships.

Languages :
English speakers always get preference because most passengers are English speaking. For a few jobs it's preferable to know a second language (like French, German, Italian or Spanish).

Personal Qualities :
You'll need to know your work inside out, be service orientated, polite, friendly and adaptable to stand the best chance of getting a job!

Some of the Jobs on Board Ship to Choose From :

(See Our Directory of Jobs for Further Details)

Ship's Officer	Ship's Rating
Carpenter	Electrician
Plumber	Painter
Maintenance Engineer/Fitter	Hotel Manager
Assistant Hotel Manager	Personnel Officer
Secretary	Cashier
Telephone Operator	Clerk
Post Office Clerk	Receptionist
Journalist	Printer
Security Officer	Hotel Manager
Chief Steward	Cabin Steward
Bellboy	Cleaner
Laundry Hand	Catering Manager
Head Chef	Sous Chef
Restaurant Manager	Assistant Restaurant Manager
Restaurant Waiter	Wine Waiter
Buffet Supervisor	Kitchen Porter
Dishwasher	Bar Manager
Barman	Bar Waiter
Cellarman	Cruise Director
Assistant Cruise Director	Host/Hostess
Travel Agent	Tour Guide
Singer	Dancer
Master of Ceremonies	DJ
Magician/Conjurer/Illusionist	Children's Entertainer
Children's Host/Youth Counsellor	Dance Teacher
Musician	Pianist/Organist
Comedian	Bridge/Chess/Cards Instructor
Librarian	Film Projectionist
TV Producer	Video Cameraman
Radio DJ	Lecturer/Hobbyist
Dance Teacher	Sports Instructor
Doctor	Dentist
Nurse	Nurse's Aide
Shop Assistant	Shop Manager
Photographer	Casino Manager

Casino Cashier	Croupier
Hair Salon Manageress	Hair Stylist
Beauty Therapist	Health Club Manager
Gym Instructor	Aerobic Instructor
Masseur/ Masseuse	Swimming Pool Attendant
Children's Host	Creche Assistant
Nanny/Babysitter	Tutor/Teacher

(Whatever the title, most jobs are open to men and women.)

Questions and Answers

Q. I've never worked at sea before. Can I still get a job?

A. Yes, certainly. You do not need to have worked at sea (or ever been on a ship before) to get a job on a cruise ship.

Q. I've no experience. Can I still get a job?

A. Yes, most new crew members are young and enthusiastic anyway. But do please get SOME good experience, on land, in the type of work you wish to do first.

Q. Can you guarantee me a job?

A. Unfortunately not. But if you follow our instructions and get in touch with the employers in our Directory you'll stand the best chance possible.

Q. How long before I get offered a job?

A. It varies so much. Some people strike lucky with their first few applications, but don't bank on it. You MUST be determined and keep applying month after month after month if you want to be successful.

Q. What will happen if I get offered a job?

A. First, you'll probably be offered a short contract to work on a named ship. Once you're in you're quite likely to be asked back - If not, it's much easier to find your next job. However, you might have several work-less (and pay-less) months before your next contract starts.

Q. Is it safe?

A. Yes. Most cruise ships are superbly maintained, captained and equipped. Accidents are extremely rare. If it wasn't safe, why would so many people pay so much to cruise?

Q. And finally, what if I'm seasick?

A. Not many people are seasick on a cruise ship. Cruise ships nowadays are fully stabilised using a system of computer-controlled fins which are hidden away below the waterline. The ride is pretty smooth, even in quite rough seas. If you are seasick you'll soon get over it, and allowances are made for new crew members to get their 'sealegs' anyway.

Some More Good Advice to Take Heed Of ....

In the rest of this book I'm going to tell you everything you need to know about finding vacancies, preparing your application, sending in your application, and passing interviews too! So, I suggest you tackle the book like this :

1. Read each chapter carefully. Don't make any applications until you have read everything.

2. When you're happy that you understand what you have to do, start preparing your application letters and forms etc. Take time to get this right.

3. Look for as many opportunities as possible. I'll show you how in the pages of this book. Make up your own list of contacts.

4. Start making your applications. You can work on this at your own pace.

5. Keep at it! You might need to apply to the same employers several times before they take you on!

I'd be very surprised if the vast majority of people reading this book now wouldn't be able to do some sort of job on a cruise ship. At the end of the day, remember that the people who work on cruise ships are only the same as those who work on land - BUT THEY'RE HAVING A GREAT TIME DOING IT! Of course, it's not always easy to convince an employer. But if you can, you're in. And here's how .... !

THE WORLD'S TOP 10 CRUISE LINES

1.	Cunard Line, United Kingdom	(16 ships)
2.	P&O (including Princess Cruises), United Kingdom	(13 ships)
3.	Epirotiki Lines, Greece	(12 ships)
4.	Carnival Cruise Lines, USA	(11 ships) *
5.	Royal Caribbean Cruise Line, Norway	(8 ships)
6.	Renaissance Cruises, Italy	(8 ships)
7.	Holland America Line, Netherlands	(7 ships)
8.	Norwegian Cruise Line, Norway	(6 ships)
9.	Regency Cruise Line, USA	(6 ships)*
10.	Costa Cruises, Italy	(5 ships)

(Ranked according to number of ships owned.)

* Note: Although many more cruise ships sail from or operate out of Miami, Florida, the majority are **not** registered in the USA.

Notes:

Notes:

Chapter 2

HOW TO FIND THE JOBS

Before You Start ....
This is a Different World !

Before setting out to get a job on a cruise ship, it's important to remember that it's not like trying to find a normal 'nine to five' job. In many ways, it's a bit of a circus and you have to follow certain procedures, and use all sorts of round-about ways, which I'm going to tell you about here ....

For a start, very few jobs on these ships are ever advertised. I'll bet that you'll hardly ever (and probably never) see one advertised in your local paper. So where do you start and how do you hear about the vacancies? Well firstly, the reason you rarely see a position advertised is that cruise lines get so many people applying direct that they rarely need to advertise. When they do, it's usually for a highly specialist job, or a very unpopular one!

But the thing to remember is that there are loads of jobs - with hundreds on just one ship. It's estimated that there are over 100,000 jobs in the cruise business and a fair proportion of these come up for grabs on new contracts every 4-6 months. But, in a world of 5,200 million people (so I'm told), you really do have to hunt them down.

Secondly, and quite understandably, because many people would like one of these sought after jobs there's a lot of competition. You really have to go to extreme lengths to get your application noticed. If you just wait for ads. to appear and fill in a few application forms then you probably won't get a job.

So be determined - and be unconventional! (More about this later!)

Fancy a Dip In The Pool ?

When a cruise line needs more staff they simply advertise, collect the applications and select someone. Right? No ... wrong! It's not like that at all. Instead, these employers like to keep a 'pool' of would-be crew available at all times. When a vacancy does arise - perhaps they've had a particularly good week for cruise bookings - they'll call up a suitable applicant and offer them a job, possibly at quite short notice.

This has two important implications for you and I, the crew member. Firstly, it means you can apply for a job to any company at ANY TIME. Secondly it means that, if they reject you now, or ignore your application, you are not necessarily unsuitable. You have to make sure you keep applying and keep letting the recruiters know that you're ready, willing and able!

The Concessionaires and Agents -
Who They Are and What They Do ....
At this point it is worth noting that only a fraction of jobs on board cruise ships are actually obtained with cruise ship companies!

It's customary, in the cruise business, for cruise lines to rent out the right to operate various facilities to specialist companies who are known as CONCESSIONAIRES. So, hair salons, shops, casinos, health clubs, plus many other facilities, are often run not by the cruise line but by a specialist company. When you think about it, it's a sensible idea to, in effect, 'franchise out' the various retail goods or service outlets on board. A concessionaire is therefore similar to a franchisee. For example, Cunard might be good at operating ships, but they can't possibly be as good at styling hair as the famous Steiner salons.

In these instances, it's no good applying to a cruise line for a job in one of the CONCESSIONS. You must apply to the concessionaires. It can be a bit tricky finding out which jobs on board ships are with the cruise line and which are with concessionaires. To complicate things further, not every line uses concessionaires and the contracts to operate concessions can change hands at very short notice. I'll tell you about some of the main concessionaires later in the book. The cruise lines will usually tell you which they work with, if you ask.

Secondly, some cruise lines appoint employment agencies to fill some or all of their vacancies. This cuts down on their admin. work tremendously. I'll be telling you about the main agencies later and, again, if a cruise line is tied up with a particular agency, this often means that you must apply to the agency instead of (or sometimes as well as) the cruise line.

Finally, remember - if you apply to a concessionaire you'll be employed by the concessionaire not the cruise line. If you apply to an agency you'll usually be employed by the cruise line, not the agency! Don't worry, it's not as confusing as it sounds!

The Four Ways of
Finding Out About Vacancies :
1. Special Contacts
2. Employment Agencies
3. Magazine Advertisements
4. Direct Applications

Special Contacts
This may seem a very unusual method, but try it if you can. Quite simply, if you have any contacts in the cruise lines or any similar field you must try and make use of them.

OK, so your next door neighbour doesn't work for Cunard. This doesn't matter. But do you know anyone who works for a travel agent, hair salon, big store, prestigious hotel or restaurant, sports club etc.? If you do, it's always worth asking if they have any leads or contacts.

For example, a young lady who wrote to me recently wanted a job as a cabin stewardess. She mentioned her plans to her hairdresser. Through the trade 'grapevine', the hairdresser knew a couple of friends who had worked on cruise ships. A quick meeting over coffee was arranged, and the would-be stewardess walked away with the names of two people in the personnel offices of two major cruise lines! Not much maybe, but when the stewardess addressed her application to these individuals BY NAME it's easy to see why it must have rocketed her name to the top of the shortlist. (By the way, she did get the job!)

Maybe it seems unconventional, but it does work, so try it. Once you're a crew member, you'll suddenly find you have lots of friends who want to know if you can fit them in somewhere!

Note: Most people don't realise how successful job-hunting through personal contacts is. In fact, it is the most common way to find work - it may seem hard to believe but approximately 70% of jobs are secured in this way and is often referred to as "networking".

Employment Agencies
In most cases, you will not find any jobs on cruise ships handled by your Job Centre or private employment agencies in your town. OK - so it's worth asking - you never know - but not many jobs are found this way.

Instead, there are several specialist employment agencies who are hired by the cruise lines (and sometimes also the concessionaires) to advertise for, select and hire their crew members. So, it's certainly worth contacting these companies and asking.

The main cruise ship employment agencies in the UK are:
Logbridge Limited
Quest Marine Services

Their addresses are given later, together with some smaller agencies and some agencies in the USA and mainland Europe which you could try.

Most of the employment agencies get a lot of enquiries and there is a great deal of competition for the jobs they have. You'll need to be SURE that you've got the experience and qualifications they require before you apply. Usually, if you send them a CV (curriculum vitae) they'll be able to tell you if they are likely to be able to find you a job. Note: I'll be explaining more about CV's later.

Magazine Advertising

As I've said, not a great many cruise ship vacancies are advertised as such. But, it is still a method you should try. The main advantage here is that if an employer is needing to advertise a job it must be something they either need to fill quickly, or are having difficulty finding a suitable person for. So your chances of getting a job which is formally advertised are quite a bit higher than the other methods.

You'll note I say magazines. Because very few of these jobs are ever advertised in newspapers. If you wish, you might look at the major daily newspapers (such as 'The Guardian', 'Daily Express', 'Daily Mail', 'The Independent', 'Daily Telegraph' - and their Sunday editions), but don't expect very many vacancies to appear.

The vacancies that are advertised are usually in specialist trade magazines - the type of publication that is read by those in a particular job or activity. For example, jobs in hair and beauty salons on cruise ships appear in 'Health and Beauty Salon'. And, if you've got a flair for entertaining and want to work on a cruise ship you might find something suitable in 'The Stage'.

I suggest you try the following magazines:

Trade and Professional Magazines
Which May Have Job Advertisements :

Administrator	British Baker
British Journal of Photography	British Printer
Caterer and Hotelkeeper	Hair
Hair and Beauty Salon	Hairdressers' Journal International
Litho Week	Music Week
Nursing Times	Nursing Mirror
Office Secretary	Overseas Jobs Express
PM Plus (Personnel)	Personnel Management
Printing World	Retail Jeweller
Screen (Media)	Shipping World and Shipbuilder
The Engineer	The Freelance (Journalism)
The Photographer	The Stage
Travel Trade Gazette	Video Trade Weekly

As the majority of these are specialist magazines, you may not find them at your local newsagent (although if you *do* require them you will be able to order them). However, because they don't have cruise ship vacancies every week or month I wouldn't advise going to the expense of ordering them or taking out a subscription. But I do recommend that you visit your local large town or city library (go to the Periodicals Library, if there is one) perhaps once a month, and spend an hour or so checking for job ads. If the magazines you want are not on display you may need to ask the librarian to get them out for you.

Overseas Jobs Express : The Overseas Jobs Express newspaper is really the only newspaper or magazine which usually has a few cruise line jobs advertised in every issue. It appears every fortnight. Their address is : Premier House, Shoreham Airport, Sussex, BN43 5FF

Some examples of the magazine advertisements you might see are as follows :

GIFT SHOP ASSISTANTS. Large cruise ship. Male or female. Preferably with a minimum of two years' experience in cosmetics, jewellery or similar. Apply to : XXXXX.

FOR A LUXURY CRUISE SHIP. WAITERS REQUIRED. You will need a sound knowledge of first class table service, plus a basic knowledge of Cordon Bleu cuisine and wines. Minimum age 20. Preference will be given to those with experience of working in a 4 or 5 star hotel/restaurant. Please send a CV and recent photo to : XXXXX.

CHEF DE PARTIE, for a prestigious cruise ship. Minimum age 25, with at least 2 years' experience in a luxury hotel or restaurant. Must hold City & Guilds 706/1 and 706/2. Apply in writing to : XXXXX.

HAIR STYLISTS AND BEAUTY THERAPISTS. Required for cruise liner sailing in the Caribbean. Must be of pleasant appearance and personality with working knowledge of leading beauty products. CV and Photo to : XXXXX.

Direct Applications

I do strongly advise that you use all the methods I have explained above. But, really, all three of these aren't enough in themselves. To stand a reasonable chance of getting a job you must make what I call DIRECT APPLICATIONS.

The idea of making direct applications is fairly straightforward. Quite simply, you write and introduce yourself to companies who are in the cruise business and who it is reasonable to assume will have jobs available - even if they are NOT CURRENTLY ADVERTISING VACANCIES. Tell them about yourself and ask if they have a job for you!

This method may seem unconventional but it is the way things are done. As I've said before, many companies never advertise because they find they can fill all their vacancies from people who write in. Most potential employers are quite used to receiving such enquiries. In most cases, if the application is well presented and from the type of person they are looking to employ, they will be very pleased to consider it.

WHO to write to :
Anyone and everyone who employs crew on board cruise ships - Cruise line companies, concessionaires and agencies. Plus anyone else remotely connected with the business.

WHERE to find addresses :
With this book we provide you with a very comprehensive list of cruise line companies, concessionaires and agencies. But remember, only you can select the ones which are most appropriate to the skills and experience you can offer. That said, why not contact them all?

BUT :

Please don't send a direct application if you know you don't have the right experience for the work in question. The company won't appreciate it, and it only wastes your own time and theirs. Much better to get the experience you need and THEN make a proper application - if you follow this advice, I'm pretty sure they'll be delighted to hear from you!

Notes:

Chapter 3

HOW TO PUT TOGETHER A
WINNING APPLICATION

(Staying Out of the 'R' for Rubbish File!)

The actual application procedure for a cruise ship job is more or less the same whether you are applying for a job that is advertised, or just making a direct application etc. You might need to send in a CV, apply by letter or (for an advertised job) fill in a standard application form.

It's a good idea to prepare some of the items you'll need before you start to actually look for jobs - so you'll have time to make sure they are really perfect before you send them anywhere. Ideas for actual letters you can use follow shortly, together with a useful all-purpose letter you can copy for enquiring about the possibility of a job, and an application form to try your hand at.

First though, the golden rule is always to follow any instructions you are given very carefully. For example, if it's a vacancy you've seen advertised then BE SURE to read the 'small print' in the ad.

I do know of personnel officers who put tricky conditions in their ads. (such as stating that you must apply in your own handwriting). This is sometimes done purely as a way of filtering out applicants and by doing so, cuts down their own workload. If you don't follow these directions (for example, if you send a typed letter) they'll assume that if you can't follow simple instructions on dry land, you'll be all at sea on a cruise ship - and more often than not they'll file your letter under 'R' for rubbish!

Of course, as long as you follow these basic instructions you are quite free to prepare and present your application as you decide. And the aim should be to make it as professional as possible, whilst standing out from all the others as much as possible. Here are my suggestions ....

First - Some Things to Make Sure You Do in Your Application

When applying for any type of job, it's difficult to know what the recruiter is expecting you to write in your application. And wouldn't it be great if you knew exactly what they were looking for so you could write just that? Well, maybe YOU can't ask them. But WE can! Over the last few months I've been talking to recruiters and personnel officers and asking them this simple question :

"Just what do you look for in your applications?"

Here are some of their answers :

- "Be brief. Just give the bare essentials and don't tell me your life story, or about your passion for the sea ...", said one, " ... It just isn't necessary anyway!"

- "Emphasise your experience, as it is relevant to the job in question. Experience is more important than anything else."

- "Don't go on too much about educational and professional qualifications. Just give basic, brief details."

- "Applicants who intimate that they are more interested in free cruising than doing their job, are likely to be spotted and eliminated! The ideal applicant is one who is committed to their job and just happens to see working on a cruise ship as another way of doing it well."

- "I'm looking for enthusiasm with realism, youth with experience, and pleasant, happy people, who also show they've thought about the drawbacks of life on board a ship (such as the long hours, lack of privacy and relative insecurity)."

- " It is essential to submit a properly produced CV (curriculum vitae) - as handwritten or badly printed ones are generally discarded without even being read."

Hopefully, these answers will give you a good insight into how you should apply and also, what you should be saying in your letters of application.

A Letter of Application

A letter of application can be tricky. You must get as much as possible in, but not make it too long. Of course, there is a major advantage over just sending a CV. Unlike a CV, which is just a statement of facts, you can use a letter to build up a personal link with the reader and get REMEMBERED.

If you cover the following points, in this order, you won't go far wrong :

1. Introduce yourself. State what job you are applying for or you can do.

2. Say something about your experience. Briefly mention your current job and qualifications.

3. Say what special attributes/qualities you can offer.

4. Say why you want the job.

5. Ask for the job! Ask for an interview!

6. A final clincher is often to say how soon you could start (if you can, of course). Cruise lines like people they can call on at short notice.

Presentation :

If you have a good typewriter (or can find a good typing service) then a typed letter is always clearer and so therefore, more likely to be read than a handwritten one. However, a handwritten letter is perfectly acceptable. But use a black or blue pen on white unlined paper. Try and avoid writing any more than two sheets of A4 paper. (Write on one side only.) Never ever use your current employer's stationery or the franking machine in the post room. It looks highly unprofessional and your prospective employer will view it as stealing (which, of course, it is).

Here are examples of two letters. (Use these by all means, but it's best to adapt them so that your letter isn't exactly the same as anyone else's.) The first is a general enquiry letter, asking about the possibility of a job. The second is a suggested application letter in reply to an advertised vacancy :

Mr. B Brown   Flat1
The Shipboard Personnel Manager   Park House
The Cruise Line Ltd.   Park Street
Princess House   London
Princess Road   WC99 1AB
Anytown
Hampshire   AB1 2AB   1 May199-

Dear Mr. Smith

My name is Jane Jones. I am enquiring if you have any job
vacancies for cabin stewardesses or chambermaids aboard any
of the cruise ships which you operate.

I am 22 years of age and currently am employed as a chambermaid
in the four-star Park Hotel, Westminster. My duties include
complete responsibility for the cleaning and presentation of
eight guest suites, together with providing first class room
service on a rota basis.

My training for this job has included taking courses in Guest
Room Presentation and Room Service Skills at the Park Hotel's
Group Staff College in London. I am also presently taking an
evening class course in French.

I do feel that my experience to date would enable me to become
a useful member of the team aboard a cruise ship, and I am
very interested in taking my career in this direction. I
would be willing to consider a position in any part of the
world, and I am available to start work at two weeks' notice.

If you have any vacancies for which I would be suitable,
either now or in the future, then I would be grateful if you
would let me know.

Yours sincerely,

Jane Jones.

Mr. A. Smith
The Shipboard Personnel Manager
Crest of a Wave Concessionaires Ltd.
King House
Queens Road

Flat 1
Park House
Park Street
London
WC99 1AB

Dear Mr. Smith

I am writing to apply for the position of 'Gift Shop Associate' as advertised in the 'Overseas Jobs Express' of 30 April.

I am 24 years of age and currently employed as a sales assistant in a local High Street jewellers. Previously, I worked in the Anytown branch of H.Samuel where I trained in all aspects of the retail jewellery business.

My present job includes assisting customers, demonstrating jewellery, handling sales and orders, together with responsibilities for the display and merchandising of the window and cabinet displays.

I do feel that this experience would make me the ideal candidate for work in the gift shop of a cruise ship. I would be willing to consider a job in any part of the world, and I am available to start work at two weeks' notice.

I would welcome the opportunity of an interview at which we could discuss this position further. If there is any other information you require please do not hesitate to let me know.

Yours sincerely,

John Jones.

A CV

The use of a CV (a curriculum vitae is your 'life history') is very common in the cruise ship business. There are very few jobs where it is not either essential or advisable to have one, when applying for a job. Remember what one cruise ship recruiter said earlier in this chapter, let me remind you; he said *"It is essential to submit a properly produced CV - handwritten or badly printed CV's are generally discarded immediately."*

If you are applying for a job with a company or agency based in the USA you might be asked for a 'resume' or a 'bio' (biography). This is more or less the same as a CV.

So, if you don't already have a CV, now is the time to prepare one. If you do already have a CV, then you should take it out and look at how it could be improved or, better still, TAILORED to suit a cruise ship job, see below.

As you may know, there are several CV companies who will prepare a CV for you. We highly recommend **The Lightning Laser C.V. Co. Telephone 01372 815011.** They will professionally script and produce your CV to a very high standard, then laser print it for you on specially designed, eye-catching, heavyweight paper. Their professionally produced CV's will certainly give your application that vital 'edge' over your competitors as this company has considerable experience in producing CV's especially for the cruise ship companies.

However, if you do not want to have your CV professionally produced, the following example shows one style of CV which would be adequate for most cruise ship applications. In this case, our guinea pig is applying for a job in a gift shop concession, but the basic CV would suit any job. To produce your own version, simply keep the same headings as in the example but take out the personal details shown and place your own in their place.

CURRICULUM VITAE

Name:	Penny Anne Leach
Address:	1 The Drive Anytown Middlesex TW1 1AB England.
Telephone:	0171 123 4567
Date of Birth:	20 February 1969
Nationality:	British
Education:	1980-1985, Anytown School. O levels : English Language (B), Maths (C), History (C), Geography (C), French (C), Science (C).
Work Experience :	The Bakery Bond Street Anytown. Saturday Assistant, June 1984-October 1985. Davenports Department Store Plc, London. Sales Assistant, October 1985-April 1988. My duties included cashier work, serving the public and stock control. Designer Gift Stores Ltd., Reading. Assistant Manageress, April 1988-Present day. My responsibilities include staff management and planning work rotas, window display, cashing up and till checks, working to a budget and sales promotion. I have complete responsibility for the shop on two days of the week.
Interests & Activities:	Foreign travel, aerobics, and socialising at weekends. I also enjoy helping with fundraising at our local hospital.
Other:	I hold a St. John Ambulance First Aid Information Certificate.

Presentation :

CV'S must ALWAYS be typed. If you are going to do it yourself and you have a good typewriter or wordprocessor that's ideal, otherwise you must use a typing or CV service. NEVER submit a handwritten CV - or that'll be another entry in the recruiter's 'R' for rubbish file!

CV's should be presented in black type on white A4 paper. Use one or two sheets of A4 paper only - do not stretch to three unless you really cannot avoid it.

Cover Letters :

Another simple way to draw attention to your CV is to attach a simple covering letter. But keep it short and very simple and don't duplicate the information from the CV. You could use the following examples. The first is to use with a CV you are sending to apply for a definite vacancy. The second is for use where you are making a direct application (where no job as such exists and you are merely introducing yourself).

```
Mr. A. Smith                          Flat 1
The Shipboard Personnel Manager       Park House
The Cruise Line Ltd.                  Park Street
Princess House                        London
Princess Road                         WC99 1AB
Anytown
Hampshire                             1 May 199-
AB1 2AB

Dear Mr. Smith

With reference to your advertisement in 'Caterer and
Hotelkeeper', May 199-, please find enclosed an up to date
copy of my CV.

I would be pleased to be considered for this position and
would welcome the opportunity of an interview.

Yours sincerely,

Jane Jones.
```

```
Mr. A. Smith                          Flat 1
The Shipboard Personnel Manager       Park House
The Cruise Line Ltd.                  Park Street
Princess House                        London
Princess Road                         WC99 1AB
Anytown
Hampshire AB1 2AB                     1 May 199-

Dear Mr. Smith

I would be very interested to hear if you have any jobs
aboard cruise ships for which you feel I may be suitable.

I am pleased to enclose my CV which provides further
information on my experience and qualifications. Currently
I work as a sales assistant in a high quality jewellers.

I look forward to hearing from you.

Yours sincerely,

John Jones.
```

Notice how short, simple and straight to the point these letters are. You really don't need to send a long rambling essay. And remember this - whilst other people are sending in their long boring applications ... YOUR letter is being read not rubbished - and all because you bought 'Crews for Cruise' ... there are more tips still to come!

An Application Form

There is no specific standard type of application form found in the cruise business. Where you are required to fill one in, the form will vary according to what that particular company wants to know! Many of them are designed for use by those who are already working at sea. If so, don't be put off - the fact you are not already at sea won't usually matter, especially if you have good experience in your job.

The best advice I can give you, when faced with a form, is to get a photocopy made of it at your local library or stationery shop. Fill in the copy, then chop-it-and-change-it until you're really happy with what you've written, and there are no mistakes. Then and only then do you fill in and post the original. The original should never ever be sent with alterations or mistakes on it. The next few pages contain samples of typical forms which you could use to fill in for experience :

CRUISING CONCESSIONS LTD.
APPLICATION FOR EMPLOYMENT

Position Applied for :

Advertised in :   Reference no. :

Surname and Forenames :

Address :

Tel. (Daytime) :   (Evening) :

(If currently at sea, please give an address within the United Kingdom where we can leave a message.)

Date of Birth :

Sex : M/F

Marital Status :

Nationality :

Passport :

Number :   Issued at :   Expiry :

Present/Most Recent Employment

Name and address of present employer :

Job title :   Date started :

Ship (if applicable) :

Period of notice required :

Previous Employment

Please include any temporary, part-time and voluntary work and explain time on land, i.e.. gaps in paid employment.

From-To: Employer: Ship :   Job: Salary: Reason for leaving?

Education

From: To: School/College: Qualifications obtained
                                      (or results awaited) with grades:

Any other trade or professional qualifications :

Details of foreign languages spoken, and level :

Language: Fluent/Intermediate/Basic:

Medical History

Please give details of any conditions or illnesses for which you have required treatment by a doctor (either on an in or out patient basis) within the last five years.

Do you currently suffer from any medical condition? YES/NO

If YES please give full details. This does not necessarily invalidate your application but you should be aware that certain conditions will render you ineligible. Any offer of employment may be subject to passing a medical examination.

Next of kin, contact address and telephone number in case of emergencies :

Other Relevant Information

Please give, in your own words, any other information you think would help us to consider your application. You may wish to discuss work experience, leisure interests and provide more details about your current job.

References

Please give the names of two people to whom reference may be made with regard to this application. If possible, one should be your current or last employer.

1.

2.

We will not contact these referees prior to making an offer of employment.

IMPORTANT !

Please give the name and address of any companies we may not pass your application to (e.g. your present employer) :

DECLARATION

I declare that the information I have supplied in this application is true. I understand that if I am offered a position and that subsequently any of the information is found to be untrue then I may be subject to immediate dismissal.

Signed :   Date :

Some Other Things That Will Improve Your Chances :

Photographs

Employers will sometimes request that you send a photograph with your application. If they do, be sure to send them - If you can't be bothered or think it doesn't matter, then this could result in your application being weeded out.

However, even if a photo isn't requested, (assuming you are at least average looking or better!) send one anyway. This will help your application stand out and it's a major plus point in the case of jobs which involve contact with the public.

Usually, a passport-sized head and shoulders shot is adequate, unless they request otherwise. A photo booth picture will do SO LONG AS IT IS A GOOD ONE. Experiment with a good pose in a mirror - wear a smart blouse or shirt and tie - no T-shirts - turn your head slightly to one side - smile a little - don't grin - don't laugh - snap!

If you are applying to an agency send at least two photos so they can, if necessary, send one on to their client (the cruise line).

References

I haven't seen many cruise ship job ads. lately where you are asked to send references with your application. The main exception is the Logbridge agency who DO ask for references, exam certificates and a photo to be sent with your initial application.

So, whether or not you send references is up to you. Personally, I don't. They only clutter up your application, and may even get lost. Instead, keep them safely and take them with you to your interviews.

A good tip is to mention in your application that you have references AVAILABLE. This tells the recruiter that you're organised, and confident enough to offer them without being asked. Simply add the following line to your application letter or cover letter ....

'I have several excellent references available and would be pleased to have the opportunity to show you these.'

Incidentally, if you don't have any references, now is the time to get some. Two or three is ideal. If possible, at least one should refer to your experience in the type of work you are now applying for. You can obtain references from :

- Past Employers. These are the very best type. Don't forget any part-time jobs. Only you will know the job was just part-time! The same applies to any unpaid jobs you have done - as I suggested at the beginning of the book.

- Your School or College. These are acceptable if you have recently left school or college and so don't have much work experience.

- Friends or Associates. These never carry as much weight as the others, but are better than nothing. If possible, try and get something that refers to some work experience, even if it was just helping out at your local church or for a charity.

Certificates
By and large there's no need to send any exam certificates unless specifically requested. And, as with references, send only good copies as the originals can very easily get lost.

How to Make Your Application Stand Out a Mile !
Once you've completed all your letters, forms and CV, check them all carefully - twice. Get someone else to read them through and see that they all make sense.

Take copies for future reference. If you end up in a 'pool' it could be weeks or months before you come to interview and it's easy to forget what you said, or for things to have changed.

Pack your application package into a large, A4 sized envelope, so that it doesn't have to be folded. Use one of those card-backed ones. This will make sure it is received in tip-top condition and, again, a larger envelope stands out that little bit more.

You might even send off your application by RECORDED DELIVERY. Not because you want delivery to be recorded, but because it will help your application stand out and get noticed.

Now I'm going to pass on a clever little technique that I've used very successfully, many times - it really works and if you're feeling determined, I recommend you try it, not just for applying for work on cruise ships but in any job application. And I'd like you to run a highlighter, or mark through this next section so that you remember it for life

Very simply, you zip off a "TELEMESSAGE" (the next-day telegram service - dial 0800 190 190 to send one) to the person responsible for hiring at the company you are applying to. On the same day, you send your application in by Recorded Mail. Word the Telemessage along the lines of "Be sure to check your mail for an application from (your name). It's the Recorded item." The next morning, the personnel officer or employer will sort through his mail. Guess what he'll open first? ... Right! *Your* Telemessage - it's irresistible, believe me! After reading your urgent message, guess what he'll do next? Right again! He'll sort through for the Recorded item ... *your* application. It has worked successfully for me every single time, so it is worth considering. Of course, it does require a little coordination and extra effort and it might be worth getting up early to catch the first post, thereby ensuring your mailing gets the best possible start.

The next day, give the recipient a call, perhaps after initially checking with his/her secretary that both items were received (and you can be sure the secretary will remember, because Telemessages are not that common). Also, being an efficient secretary, she will have put your Telemessage *on top of the pile of mail*. Even if your application isn't the best, the employer is sure to be pretty impressed by your initiative! Nine times out of ten, your application will be opened and read **first** ... half the battle's won!

Alternatively, 'phone the company you are applying to three days after you expect the application to have been delivered. Say you're "just calling to make sure my letter has been received, and to see if you need any further information". In reality this is just a ploy to get your application to stand out over those applicants who do not call (99% of other applicants)! If you can, chat to the personnel officer, ask a few questions, and try and build up something of a rapport.

Little details maybe. And not always easy to do. But they do make a difference, believe me.

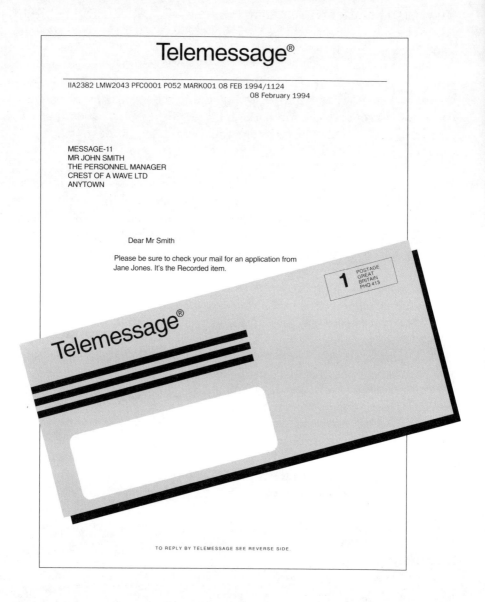

Telemessage®

IIA2382 LMW2043 PFC0001 P052 MARK001 08 FEB 1994/1124

08 February 1994

MESSAGE-11
MR JOHN SMITH
THE PERSONNEL MANAGER
CREST OF A WAVE LTD
ANYTOWN

Dear Mr Smith

Please be sure to check your mail for an application from
Jane Jones. It's the Recorded item.

Telemessage®

1 POSTAGE
GREAT
BRITAIN
PHQ 413

TO REPLY BY TELEMESSAGE SEE REVERSE SIDE.

Telemessage is a registered trademark of BT plc and is reproduced with permission of BT Message Services.

The access telephone number for Telemessage/International Telegrams is 0800 190 190.

Where to Send Your Application To ....

Don't Guess It - Name It !

You may know the name of the cruise line, concessionaire or agency - but is this enough? A very good idea is to contact the company in question and find out who is responsible for recruiting - the switchboard or receptionist will usually be perfectly happy to tell you and it has only cost the price of a 'phone call. Then, ADDRESS YOUR APPLICATION TO THEM BY NAME.

For cruise lines, it's usual to direct your correspondence to Mr/Mrs/Ms Whoever - followed by the term SHIPBOARD PERSONNEL MANAGER. This is the usual term for the head recruiter, although other titles are used too. It will mean your application gets to the right place - and make sure that it doesn't get mixed up with the ordinary, boring applications for typists and cleaners etc. at head office. So, for example, address the envelope like this :

Mr. A. Smith
The Shipboard Personnel Manager
A Cruise Line Ltd.

OR

Mrs. A. Smith
The Shipboard Personnel Manager
A Concessionaire Ltd.

OR

Miss A. Smith
The Shipboard Personnel Manager
An Employment Agency Ltd.

Be Different! : As an alternative, you might try writing to the head of the relevant department or the Chief Purser on board individual cruise ships. Write to them 'care of' the company's head office. This is a little unconventional but it can work. It by-passes all the many applications at head office thus showing initiative and making your application stand out. Many ships' officers have limited rights to hire staff (though mostly it's all controlled by head office) so it's worth a try. For example :

Mr. A. Smith
Chief Purser
S.S. Cruise Liner
c/o A Cruise Line Ltd.

There may be some delay but cruise lines do have an internal mail system where such communications are flown out to meet the ship at its next port of call.

Some More Good Advice

1. Try and set aside some time for tracking down vacancies every week. Build up a personal address book of possible employers.

2. As you locate addresses and opportunities, send off applications.

3. Keep doing this until you get replies and you are offered interviews etc. You will!

4. Keep trying. If necessary keep applying to the same companies more than once. It's quite usual.

5. Don't wait for replies before sending more applications.

You might be lucky and get a job first time; if you do, congratulations! But, you might as well be realistic and expect a lot of rejections! It happens to everyone. If you are rejected, don't worry. Here's something else I'd like to pass on to you - it gave me incredible determination.

Some years ago, I applied for a series of jobs. Each negative reply made me feel worse and worse. After the sixth rejection, I really lost heart. So much so, that I gave up applying and began to grow extremely disillusioned. Then, by chance, I ran into an old friend of mine who was in the same profession. He was euphoric at having just secured a position with a very good company. I was positively green with envy! You see I knew that I was better qualified than him and yet he had secured the job that could have been mine, dammit! I asked my friend how he had managed to get the job. He replied that he had spent two whole weeks mailing his CV to **200** different companies, and from that received 199 rejections or 'no replies'. But that didn't matter. He only got one job offer ... but one job was all he was after! And do you know why my friend got the job instead of me? Very simply, **I hadn't sent that company an application, so they didn't know I existed.**

In other words, because I had been despondent and given up hope, I failed to get the one job that I was fully qualified to do. It taught me a very valuable lesson ... **never _ever_ give up trying, and keep applying!!**

So, do keep trying. I know it can be discouraging after just two or three rejections. (Plus you have to expect that a proportion of companies won't even bother to reply to you.) But you must persist until you're offered a job or an interview. Even if a company feels it might be able to offer you a job, it may be several months before you are drawn from the pool and interviewed. I was once telephoned by a company and offered a job one YEAR after I had applied to them! They had been let down at short notice and wanted me to start immediately. This can and does happen. And this example also demonstrates the importance of making sure your details are kept on file - it's quite feasible for the person who was successful in securing the position on offer to 'drop out' for one reason or another. Then the next person in line (possibly you) is contacted urgently and offered the position. In this instance, don't be too proud to accept!

CHECKLIST

☐	Prepare your own personal list of suitable cruise lines you could apply to.
☐	Add any concessionaires you could apply to.
☐	Are there any 'special contacts' you could use?
☐	Are there any agencies you could use?
☐	Check relevant magazine ads.
☐	Prepare a letter of application.
☐	Prepare/overhaul your CV. Seriously consider having your CV professionally scripted and produced. We recommend **The Lightning Laser CV Co. Tel: 01372 815011** for help and advice.
☐	Prepare answers to application forms.
☐	Decide what follow-up techniques you could use, e.g.. 'phone calls or maybe using the telemessage technique I mentioned earlier.

Notes:

Chapter 4

THE PERFECT INTERVIEW
AND OTHER USEFUL TIPS

What You Need to Know
About Interviews ....

At this point, the aim should be to keep making enough applications until you start to get invited for interviews. Once your first interview arrives you jump a whole lot nearer to taking up your first job. Remember that, by the law of averages, if you send out enough applications some of them are BOUND to lead to interviews. If for some reason you don't get any, then look again at your letter and your CV. Maybe you should consider changing or improving them and then apply again. If at first you don't succeed, try again and again.

By and large, most cruise lines and concessionaires use a personal interview as a way of recruiting staff. If you have applied to an agency, then either the agency will interview you, or they'll pass you onto the personnel department of the cruise line. Either way, you probably won't have to go through two interviews.

The stage at which an interview is granted can vary. Most companies will pool all applicants sending a half-decent CV, then select the best and interview them when a job becomes available. Others will interview you straight away, and then pool your application.

Finally, if you are applying to a foreign company, then don't worry that your interview appointment will be 3.30pm on Thursday - in Miami! A good many foreign companies who recruit in the UK have an agent here whom they trust to interview on their behalf.

Countdown to Interview Day

It is very important to prepare for the interview in advance. Once done, that preparation can last for many interviews. And if you do have to go through dozens of interviews before getting your job - so what? - think of each one as a great way of preparing for the next!

Firstly, find out exactly where the interview is going to be held, how you'll get there and how long it will take. You may need to stay overnight nearby. Try and arrive in the local area at least an hour before the arranged time. Find a cafe and sit down with a coffee and take time to compose yourself.

Don't forget to take these items with you :

- A copy of the CV you sent to this company. If things have changed since then, be ready to mention this (especially if you have gained extra experience).

- Copies of your application letter/forms. Crib-up on them before to make sure your answers to any questions tally with what you have written!

- Any relevant certificates or references.

- Examples of your work, where relevant and practical. For example, if you are a musician bring a video or audio tape of your performance. If you are a chef, bring some menus. This shows initiative, and recruiters are on the lookout for people with a little extra spark or initiative.

In most cases, you'll have to pay any travel and accommodation costs yourself. I don't know of any companies who will cover your expenses.

Dress to Impress, or Maybe Not ?

Dress is an important matter for any interview and you'll need to give some thought beforehand as to what you should wear. Generally, this will depend on whether you expect to be working with the passengers on board ship or not.

If you're anticipating working with the passengers, you should dress to your BEST possible standard, because the recruiters will definitely have a preference for people with a pleasing, well groomed appearance. So a suit for men, and very smart outfit for women, is called for. Hair and make up should be done to the very best standard you can.

On the other hand, if you're NOT in a passenger-contact role you don't want to be too dressy. A simple shirt and tie, blazer and trousers for men will be perfectly adequate, with neatly cut hair, and freshly shaved. Women should opt for a blouse and skirt or similar, with simply styled hair and neat but basic make up. This isn't to say that smart appearance isn't important, but you don't want to look unused to hard work! May I just point out, that jeans and T-shirts are taboo!

Finally, pack all your CV's, references and other documents into a wallet or folder - that will then convey a very smart, efficient and presentable picture!

Your Secret Weapon -
Make the Interview Fit the Company !

Generally, I think you will find that the cruise line recruiters are much more human than you might think. Some of those I know of are even quite friendly! If anything, the concessionaires and agencies are more up-tight - they're all too aware that they are constantly under the beady eye of the cruise line, and desperate not to get caught out by selecting the wrong type of people.

The best piece of advice I can give you is always to THINK ABOUT THE TYPE OF CRUISE LINE YOU HOPE TO BE WORKING FOR.

Here are 5 Hot Interview Tips

1.   Always arrive on time, don't be late. If you are, you'll be flustered; and making excuses about the traffic or late trains will not go down well. I always arrive at least an hour before the allotted time, sit down in a cafe, have a coffee and think about what I'm going to say during the interview etc.

2.   Always remember these three vital points when attending an interview: presentation, presentation and presentation! In other words, the way you look, act and put yourself across is of primary importance. The way you look will speak volumes about you. I've already mentioned your dress code, but I must stress that you will need to look immaculate on the day.

3.   Don't ramble, babble or prattle on, just for the sake of talking. Engage your brain before opening your mouth. Look the interviewer straight in the eye. Try to overcome nervousness and be assertive. Relax, smile and try to project your personality. A sense of humour is fine, but don't try cracking jokes - they may fall flat and leave you with egg on your face! I remember an interview I once attended; the interviewer obviously had a sense of humour and we got on really well. Finally he said "John, I hope you won't mind me asking, but are you gay?" I replied, "Give me a kiss and I'll tell you!" ... I got the job. Luckily, my sense of humour on this occasion went down well ... but it could have backfired - so do be careful.

4.   You might meet other applicants on the day of your interview while you're waiting to be shown in. Don't be disheartened or overawed by the competition, even if they appear to be better qualified than you. It's quite possible that you will get the job ahead of someone else just because (for example) you have a sparkling personality and the others haven't. Or you may just 'fit in' with the job requirements or perhaps appear to 'mix well' with others; after all, qualifications

aren't everything ... and recruiters are looking for people with bubbly dispositions, and a great persona. So be **confident**, tell yourself that you will secure the position on offer and if you believe it yourself, you'll convey your confidence to the interviewer; this really does work!

5.   Interviewing and being interviewed is an art. If you know what an interviewer is looking for, you can 'arm' yourself accordingly. I remember one instance when the interviewer just looked at me as if waiting for me to speak. Perhaps he thought that I would start prattling and maybe dig a hole for myself to fall into head first. If this should happen to you, just smile sweetly and wait for him/her to continue. As I've already said, most interviewers are human; on the whole, they're polite and courteous, but some seem to delight in 'putting you on the spot' waiting for you to dive into that hole once again. If possible, try to 'steer' the interview round to a conversational level that will make you feel comfortable. You can do this by perhaps answering a question and then asking one yourself; in this way, you can slightly control the conversation without making it obvious that you're doing so.

Some cruise lines, like Cunard Royal Viking, are traditional cruise lines, offering traditional high-class cruising to wealthy, middle and upper class passengers, who are mostly middle aged or even quite elderly. Others, like Carnival, are fun cruise lines, which attract average-income holidaymakers on party cruises, serving up non-stop fun and entertainment. They attract more young couples, singles and families with children.

So - It doesn't take a genius to guess that these different cruise lines need different types of people to work on board, especially if you'll be in contact with the passengers. You will considerably boost your chances of success by approaching the interview to suit. An informal, cheerful, chatty approach might take you into difficult waters at a Cunard interview, whereas the Carnival recruiter might see you as a real life and soul of the party, and just perfect for the job!

Our Directory of Employers will give you some hints and tips. However, I'd advise you to FIND OUT what you can about your prospective employer before the interview. (You can do this free by studying the respective cruise lines' brochures at your local travel agents.)

Finally, in either case, try to relax, just a little. Don't worry about being nervous, as most interviewers are trained to allow for this. Also, be ready for the panel interview. In many cases there'll be somebody from the personnel department (weighing you up as an employee) and somebody from the relevant shipboard department (who knows your job inside out and is out to check your competence).

Some Questions You May Be Asked
(Don't get caught out!)

Again, it's always difficult to know what you might be asked at any interview. In this section we'll look at some of the most popular questions (and suggest how your ideal answer might go!).

Q. OK, Miss Smith, could you tell us about yourself?

A. The usual, impossible to answer, wide-open question. Whilst you'll need to think beforehand of a few interesting, worthwhile things you can say, the recruiters are probably probing into your work experience here. Be sure to EMPHASISE (not exaggerate) aspects of your past jobs which relate to the cruise line job.

Q. Could you tell us about your current job?

A. Do just that. Again, emphasise your experience. For example, if you're a secretary applying for a job as Purser's Receptionist, you'll need to emphasise how your job has brought you into contact with the PUBLIC.

Q. Have you ever worked on board a ship before?

A. It's OK to say no. Simply say that you have thought carefully about the way of life involved and think it would suit you. If you have ever spent time working away from home before then it will help to mention that.

Q. Have you always wanted to work at sea?

A. You don't have to say yes. It's probably best to say that you see a cruise line position as just another very good way of working in a job you enjoy.

Q. So, what problems do you think you might encounter doing your job at sea?

A. Think about this beforehand. Never say 'none'. In addition DO say that you expect to carry out your duties to the same high standard at sea as you would on land.

Q. So what would you do if ....

A. At this point the recruiter will probably conjure up a tricky hypothetical question to which there's no easy answer. The safest reply is to answer as the question above. (I once heard that an Assistant Purser was pressed on what he would do if a nervous and hysterical passenger on a transatlantic crossing suddenly appeared and demanded to be set down on dry land! Stewards can expect to be asked more conventional questions, such as your course of action if a passenger finds a fly in his soup!)

Q. What problems do you think you might experience living at sea for long periods?

A. Do show that you appreciate the drawbacks, e.g. long hours, lack of privacy and insecurity of employment. Point out that you aren't expecting a free cruise, though you think you'll enjoy the lifestyle.

Q. Are you gay?

A. Quite a likely question, especially for lines based in the USA. Not that cruise lines are any more or less discriminatory than other employers but they do worry that gay communities may dominate particular ships.

Q. What do you know about Rustbucket Cruise Lines and why did you choose to apply to us?

A. Try and memorise some basic points, especially what the line is best known for, e.g.. luxury cruising, good cuisine or service etc. If you've been applying for every job under the sun it's difficult to answer the second part of this question, but try and point out how well you think you will fit in with the style of cruising the company offers.

And what YOU should ask THEM ....

It happens in every interview. And almost everybody (me included) gets caught out. We all know the question's coming .... Something along the lines of 'Well, is there anything you'd like to ask about this job?'.

Now, it's all too easy to say 'no' and get out of that interview hot seat as soon as possible. But please, please never do this. It's so much better to think of some relevant and worthwhile questions to ask. Even if you don't actually need to know anything, it is worth asking something so that it makes you look more interested, and it may help to get you remembered.

You might ask about the following :

Q. What sort of passengers does Rustbucket Cruise Lines attract?

This will help you plan your own answers, and is good to know for any future applications.

Q. How long is the original contract and is it likely to be renewed?

If you are fortunate enough to receive more than one job offer you might decide on the basis of the length of the contract.

Q. What rate of pay are you offering?

Never be afraid to ask about money. In some cases it could be much lower than you might think. You might want the job badly but there's no reason why you should work for peanuts.

Q. What are the chances for promotion?

It makes you look keen and enthusiastic, though often the opportunities are limited and so it doesn't pay to be too ambitious. There's only room for one captain!

Q. What methods do you use in such-and-such?

It's always a good idea to show an interest in the way the cruise line runs. Your question will need to be related to your type of work. For example, if you are applying for the position of steward, you might ask if silver service is operated. If a beauty therapist, you might enquire about the particular treatments and brands used in the salon. When asking these questions, try and strike a balance. Don't sound as if you can afford to pick and choose employers, but don't be too ready to accept anything you are offered either. Remember, above all, it's a chance to strike up some sort of rapport with the interviewer and so get remembered.

Trade Tests .... Be Prepared !

Most cruise line employers hire on the basis of an interview alone. Formal selection tests as such are rare. However, do be prepared to undergo what is known as a 'trade test'. This might be at a later date, but it could also come, quite out of the blue, at or after the interview. For example :

- If you've stated that you speak a foreign language, it may be tested by a random question, or conversation with a native speaker.

- If you're seeking employment as a waiter, you may be asked to serve lunch in the director's dining room.

- If you're seeking employment as a beauty therapist, you may be asked to give a beauty treatment.

- If you're seeking employment as an entertainer you may be asked to do a 'turn'.

- If you're seeking employment as one of the cruise or social staff you might be given five minutes to prepare, then asked to give a 'welcome aboard, we're very pleased to see you' speech to a make-believe audience of new passengers.

So, again, don't be caught out!

Following Up (Highly Recommended)

It's extremely unlikely, even if you've given the best interview ever, that you'll be given a job there and then. Most likely, you'll be informed of the outcome by letter, a few days later. If this isn't a definite job it will be a placing into a pool, awaiting a vacancy.

AND THIS IS A GREAT CHANCE TO BOOST YOUR CHANCES EVEN FURTHER!

In the first place, it's a good idea to write a short note of thanks. Or, alternatively, telephone the personnel department and ask 'if there is anything else you would like to know'.

The only purpose of this is to get your name remembered over and above those applicants who don't follow up (most people!).

One young lady who wrote to me used a particularly clever tactic. After always making sure her interview was the last one before lunch ('phoning to change it beforehand) she would quite determinedly ask, at the interview, if it was possible for her to have lunch in the staff restaurant. After pointing out the distance she had travelled, very few interviewers would turn down her request. At the very least, this was a chance to get noticed. And a good few interviewers would actually escort her to lunch, giving an unrivalled opportunity to strike up a rapport.

Whilst I'm not necessarily saying that you could use this method successfully, it does show what can be done if you try - and I'm sure you will appreciate how such things would help to get you noticed! Once again, I'm trying to demonstrate to you how you can succeed over others who have not read this book. Try to be a little unconventional - if it means using a little trick like this, then why not!

What to do if you FAIL

You must be prepared to receive some rejections. All I can say is that this doesn't necessarily mean you did badly. It may be that you simply didn't 'click' with the interviewer on this occasion.

The best advice is that you must KEEP APPLYING. By the law of averages there is just bound to be an occasion when you do 'click' with the interviewer. Then you're in!

If you're clever, this failure can be used to boost your chances of success next time :

- Call and ask why you weren't successful. Employers usually state that they reserve the right not to give a reason to unsuccessful applicants. But they often WILL if asked on an off-the-record basis.

- Call and ask if your details can be 'kept on file' (I've already stressed the importance of this in an earlier chapter). If they agree, this usually means you succeeded at interview but the job happened to be awarded to someone else, perhaps by chance.

- Call and ask if there are any other similar jobs you would be considered for. It's not unlikely, in this business, that you accidentally applied for the wrong job, i.e.. one that was too senior or junior.

- Apply again, for the same job, in a few months. (Because even if your application is kept on file, this is unlikely to be done for more than six months unless you apply again.)

- Apply again for totally different jobs. For example (assuming you have the experience) you could apply to be a restaurant steward, a cabin steward, *and* a bar steward. The employer won't consider you for the other jobs UNLESS YOU APPLY.

- Look at your letter and CV again (is your CV really up to scratch??) maybe you should try totally different versions. For example, is your CV geared towards applying for work on board cruise lines??

IF YOU STILL CAN'T GET A JOB - then in 95% of cases, lack of experience is probably the reason. So, look for land-based jobs which will give you that experience. Then, in six months or a year, start the whole procedure again.

When You SUCCEED

Congratulations! Hopefully, if you have followed all the advice in this book, you should, sometime, receive an offer you won't want to refuse!

But - please remember - it's not all plain sailing from here on. You might still be placed in a pool and have several weeks or months to wait before you are assigned to a ship.

.... During this period KEEP APPLYING FOR OTHER JOBS. Due to a change in plans, the offer might not be made final. This is quite common. In the meantime you might get a better offer.

.... During this period DO NOT RESIGN FROM YOUR CURRENT JOB. Do not do this until you have signed a contract with the new employer and, preferably, been told of your ship, start date and port of joining.

Notes:

Chapter 5

PAY, CONTRACTS, BENEFITS
AND OTHER USEFUL INFORMATION

What You Need to Know About Contracts

Every reputable company will provide a contract of employment which they will ask you to sign, and abide by. Read this carefully - even take professional advice if you wish. However, I've never seen a contract that isn't completely fair and reasonable to the employee. Reputable cruise lines have no interest in tying their workers down with unreasonable contracts. If you're unhappy then your unhappiness will only rub off on the passengers.

These are the four main points to check :

- Who is my employer? - How long does my contract last? - The rate of pay. - Other benefits available.

Who Is My Employer ?

Depending on the type of job, you could be employed by the cruise line, a concessionaire, or an agency. In each case the contract will be similarly worded, but note that if you work for a concessionaire or agent and their contract with the cruise line expires (or their contract is terminated, which can occasionally happen) you'll probably be out of a job too.

A very few jobs on board cruise ships (such as some hairdressers) do not have employee status. Instead you are hired as a freelancer, probably with no fixed contract period, and simply on one week or one month's notice.

How Long Does My Contract Last ?

Most cruise ship crew divide into 'career' and 'contract' personnel. Career personnel (such as the Captain, the officers and engineering staff) are hired on an indefinite basis, like most employees on dry land. Most other crew are hired on a fixed contract period.

There is no set contract period. It depends solely on what was offered at the interview (remember - I told you to ask!). It is unlikely you will be offered less than four months. Six or eight months is quite usual. Rarely will you be hired for more than twelve months at a time.

At the end of a contract, assuming you've worked well, you will usually be invited to come back again for another contract period. But the important thing to note is that this is NEVER guaranteed. If the cruise line don't like you, or even if they do but they are short of bookings, you will be out of a job.

Information About Pay Aboard Ship

There is no standard rate of pay. Rates of pay vary widely between jobs, companies and ships. Generally, however, for most contract jobs they are not high - you will almost always get a similar, better paid job on dry land. The pleasures of a life on the ocean wave are supposed to compensate for the not-so-high pay (and they certainly do!)

As most of what you need on board is available free or very cheaply, and there's not actually much to spend money on, you'll still probably manage to save a nice sum.

Depending on the type of job, you'll be paid by :

SALARY ONLY	This is most usual for administrative personnel and deck/engineering crew.
Or :	
SALARY + TIPS	Most crew who serve the passengers directly (cabin, restaurants and bar stewards etc., but not social staff) receive a basic salary but are also tipped.
Or :	
SALARY + COMMISSION	Most crew who are involved in a sales function (such as shop staff) receive a basic salary and a commission or sales bonus.

- All About Tips

In most jobs where you are eligible for tips, your basic salary will be intentionally low with the expectation that it will be boosted by tips. A few cruise lines have a 'no tipping necessary' policy. This was pioneered by the Ukrainian CTC Lines. However, companies such as Cunard Crown have now introduced this. In such cases your basic salary will be higher to compensate.

Tips can often be surprisingly large, and often EXCEED your salary. Most cruise passengers are American and tip automatically. If you give them especially good service they will often double or treble the tip!

Many cruise lines give their passengers a suggestion for the minimum tip they should pay you. As it's very bad form to be seen not to meet or exceed this you can usually expect at least the minimum. For example, most lines suggest that passengers should tip at least US$8.00 per day, to be divided between cabin and restaurant stewards.

Some cruise lines will pay you what is known as a 'guaranteed gratuity'. This is paid by way of a levy on the fare paid by the passenger which is then added automatically to your basic salary.

Depending on the individual ship you will either keep all your own tips or pool them with colleagues in the same job.

- Here's What You Might Earn

Most big cruise lines today pay their crew in US dollars, but it could be any currency and you should make sure this is stated in your contract. The following are examples of some current rates of pay.

Cabin Steward. Minimum US$275 per month plus tips.

Restaurant Steward. Minimum US$500 per month plus tips.

Tips for both the above jobs may take the monthly pay to US$2,000, or even US$3,000 per month in some circumstances.

A typical cabin steward will service 18 two-berth cabins as part of a two-person team. On an average cruise line, he or she will receive US$4.00 minimum per passenger per day in tips (as recommended by the cruise line). So, on a seven day cruise this amounts to :

18 cabins x 2 passengers each x 7 days x US$3.75 per day x shared between two = US$504 per week.

Casino Croupier. Minimum US$500 per week. Possibly some tips.

Entertainer (singer/dancer etc.). Minimum US$500 per week.

Gym Instructor. Typically US$12,000 per year, or part thereof.

Gift Shop Assistant. Typically US$10,000 per year, plus commission of .5% on sales. (Commission average US$225 on a seven day cruise.)

Restaurant Manager. Up to US$60,000 per year.

Information About Benefits and Life Afloat

Like pay, the benefits available to cruise ship crew also vary very much from company to company. Generally, crews divide into those of 'officer' status and 'rating' status. Only those of officer status are permitted to use all the ship's facilities and mix with the passengers. Ratings are not allowed either privilege.

Most management and other important positions carry officer status. This includes the entertainment staff, cruise or social department staff, the photographers etc., and these people will be welcome in the bar, gym, nightclub or pool. But if you're a steward (even quite a senior one) you'll be a rating and these places will be off limits.

Staff working for concessionaires fall somewhere between these two points. For example, as a hair stylist or shop assistant, you should usually be able to socialise together in the bars, disco and gym, but NOT fraternise with the passengers, or go anywhere near the passenger staterooms (cabins), nor use the casino and this might be just as well!!!

Needless to say, there's a certain amount of rule bending - and a fair bit of tiptoeing around the passenger corridors in the dead of night too - and I should know - I was caught on more than one occasion!! Most cruise lines are fairly tolerant though, so long as the passengers don't complain. (And, believe me, some of them complain if such goings-on DON'T happen!)

In any case, most cruise lines provide good facilities for the crew, although they will not be quite as luxurious as passenger facilities. These, and other standard benefits, might include :

- All meals free. Usually in unlimited quantities and of a very high standard - watch your waistline!

- Free accommodation on board. Usually in small two berth cabins (occasionally four berth) with either private or shared bathrooms. Sometimes you will share a cabin with another member of the same sex and possibly in the same profession or rating. Staff of concessions may be charged for accommodation, but rates are very low and often paid by the employer anyway.

- Free laundry for uniforms, and large discount for personal clothing.

- Discounted crew shop for everyday items.

- Discounted crew bar (quantity limited).

- Discounts on any passenger facilities you are allowed to use, e.g. duty free shops.

- Crew gym, video room, library, games room, possibly a swimming pool.

- Return travel to/from the ship. If you join or leave the ship away from a UK port, you will usually receive free air travel outward and home. (Very few cruise ships actually sail from the UK.)

BUT :

- It's worth noting there is no paid holiday on board, no matter how long the cruise. Often there is not even a regular day off. Many crew work seven day weeks and receive only occasional days off.

- There is no guaranteed free time in every port.

- There is no paid holiday. Your time back at home is usually unpaid except in exceptional circumstances, such as refitting of the ship.

And remember :

The social life is one of the most enjoyable parts of working on a cruise ship but you do have to make the effort to join in. Not that it's hard - activities include cabin or deck parties (sometimes lasting several days - and I could write a book about these alone!), quizzes and contests (some of them quite bizarre I can tell you!), beach parties, pub crawls and excursions or expeditions ashore!

Information About Wages and Income Tax
Your wages will be paid either weekly or monthly and can be credited either to a UK bank account or your account at the Purser's office from where you can withdraw it in cash. Some employers hold back a percentage of your salary which they will pay over (often with a bonus) at the end of your contract. This is to discourage you from jumping ship on an island paradise like Tonga or Antigua! (It has been known!)

The special status of most cruise ships means that they can pay your wages without having to deduct income taxes like a land based employer has to. However, whether or not you must then pay tax over to the tax man depends, not on the ship, but on YOU. You can only avoid paying British income tax if you work at sea for at least one full tax year (which runs April 6 to April 5 each year) and do not come back to the UK (for visits etc.) for a period exceeding six months. If not, you are still supposed to pay income tax on your wages AND your tips or commission even if it was actually earned outside the UK.

Many cruise lines offer TAX FREE PAY. This means they pay it to you without deducting tax. It does not necessarily mean you do not have to pay tax! Although many crew do not declare their income, the proper procedure is to inform your local Inland Revenue office that you are going to work at sea and for how long. They will then be able to tell you what your position is.

Information About Social Security and Health Insurance
Check carefully into what arrangements are made for social security and health insurance.

Most cruise lines provide free medical attention on board ship for all their crew, and insurance cover for treatment in the nearest land-based hospital should it ever be necessary. If you work for a concessionaire, agency or are self-employed, then do check, as this may not be provided free.

In any case, cruise line employers do not deduct National Insurance contributions from your wages. Good news on one hand - bad news on the other, because your UK National Insurance record will be left incomplete.

Think about this carefully. Because if you don't pay these contributions and then need to claim state benefits later on, you might find that your friendly local DSS office won't pay up! Many a crew member finds it necessary to claim unemployment benefit etc. to cover the gap between finishing one contract and starting another. Talk to your fellow crew members and ask their advice on the best ways to deal with these matters.

You can continue to pay National Insurance voluntarily while you are away if you wish and so ensure you stay fully entitled to state benefits. Contact your local DSS office for details.

Information About Passports, Visas and Work Permits
Before taking up your job, you must have a valid passport. Get a full British passport, not a British Visitor's passport. Preferably, this should last beyond the end of your contract, so renew it early if necessary. (In fact, it's a good idea to check this before you even start to apply - if you're offered a last-minute vacancy you'll have to be ready to move fast!)

Usually, passports are lodged with the Purser once joining the ship. They can then be inspected by Customs and Immigration as necessary and, in many cases, you never need to see them again. This also gives the cruise line the added security that you won't 'jump ship'.

Whether you'll need visas and work permits depends, not on the country you are based in, not on the country in which the cruise line is based in, nor countries visited, but on the SHIP'S COUNTRY OF REGISTRY. Most ships are registered in countries where few problems (such as work permits) arise. Your employer will help with this anyway.

Because of strict immigration controls, it is extremely difficult to get a job on a US registered ship. To skirt around this problem, nearly all US cruise lines cleverly register their ships abroad, usually in countries such as Panama!

Finally, What is a Slave Ship ?
The term 'slave ship' is used by ship's crew to describe a ship which doesn't offer at least the minimum pay and conditions I've outlined here. For example, SOME of the ships sailing off the coast of Florida and offering their passengers non-stop gambling (which is illegal in most US states) fall into this category. (Note; This is perfectly LEGAL and many of the reputable cruise lines offer cruises for just the same reasons.)

Whilst you'll hopefully never encounter a slave ship (we haven't knowingly listed any of these ships in our Directory of Employers) it's as well to be aware that they do exist. If you are ever offered less than a minimum fair wage, or hear of crew talking about a slave ship, it's best to give it a wide berth - pun intended.

Some More Good Advice

If you only use one piece of information from this chapter, let it be this : You MUST keep applying .... to the same and different companies .... if you seriously want to get a job.

Remember, you're not looking to work in a shop or an office where there are literally thousands of potential employers. There are only so many cruise lines and so many concessionaires. You can't apply to them all just once. So, keep applying (unless they tell you not to, which is very rare). Most companies WILL be quite prepared to consider you again in the future.

People do sometimes write and tell me that after sending off their applications to cruise lines, they don't get the response they had hoped for. Should this happen to you, I must reiterate that either you don't have sufficient experience for the position you are applying for, or you must re-think your CV. I cannot stress the importance of sending in a good CV. Is yours really relevant to the job you're after? Is it properly and professionally scripted and well produced? Are you sending a neatly typed application letter with your CV? And finally, remember, if at first you don't succeed, you must try again and again. Your determination to succeed only depends on **you!**

Cruise lines often show me some of the applications they receive; and you may find this hard to believe but after spending good money on purchasing this book, people will still not heed the advice contained in these pages. For example, I have just seen a batch of applications that were sent to one personnel manager. The **majority** of applicants sent in **badly produced CV's**; handwritten application letters that had spelling mistakes, words crossed out, or were written on scrappy pieces of lined notepaper (never use lined paper) and generally were completely sub-standard. So my question to you now is this. Are you going to waste money sending in sub- standard applications, or are you going to go about applying for work in the correct manner? It's up to you!

If after applying in the correct manner you still don't get the response you would like, then maybe you should try being slightly more aggressive or unconventional in your approach to getting a job. For example, I recently heard of one enterprising young man who desperately needed a job. He designed and had printed hundreds of cards with his details and qualifications on. Then he booked a train ticket to London and spent a week touring the capital, placing his cards under the windscreen wipers of every prestigious parked car that he thought might belong to a company director - Rolls Royces, Bentleys, Jaguars etc. Within one month that man started a new job. And I bet I know why; his idea showed he possessed initiative and recruiters and personnel managers like to employ people with initiative, drive and the ability to work well unsupervised.

Perhaps this little example will enable you to develop your own ideas of how to get ahead of your rivals in the hunt for a job. Mind you, I wouldn't suggest sticking cards under the windscreen wipers of cruise ships if I were you, I don't think that would work somehow!

CHECKLIST

☐ Interview preparation?

☐ Copies of all letters, CV's and forms to hand?

☐ Find out about the company. Decide on an approach.

☐ Prepare answers to likely questions.

☐ Prepare questions to ask.

☐ Prepare for 'trade tests'.

☐ After interview :

☐ Follow up.

☐ Failed? What action to take?

☐ Success? Check contract details before signing.

Notes:

Chapter 6

DIRECTORY OF JOBS
including the different 'Departments'

What Jobs Are Needed, Where, How Many, and How and Where to Apply ....

The range of jobs on a cruise ship is generally much vaster than you could ever imagine. As I said at the beginning of the book, a cruise ship is literally a floating hotel. It offers every type of work that a hotel requires, plus much more too!

This section gives you JOB PROFILES for all the jobs available on a typical ship, together with the basic requirements you must meet, and how to go about getting each one.

When you read these job profiles, you will probably find that there are several jobs you could do. So why not apply for them all? Whilst there's no point in applying for a job you know nothing about, it's quite possible that you will be able to apply for several types of work listed here.

If, for example, you intend to become a restaurant steward, then it is sensible to apply for suitable cabin steward and bar steward jobs as well. So, if you fail to find one type of work, just pick another from this section and start the whole process again!

The Hierarchy On a Cruise Ship

The crew on any cruise ship are organised into a fairly strict hierarchy. In fact, it's a system that's not too far removed from that found on navy ships and, whilst not always logical, its customs are steeped in tradition.

Firstly, crew divide into 'career' personnel and 'contract' personnel. Most crew on the ship sailing and management side are merchant mariners, making a life on the sea, and as such they are considered a cut above everyone else! The contract staff are mostly doing a dry-land job which just happens to be on a ship - so still, in the eyes of the mariners - 'land-lubbers', no matter how long they've been at sea!

Whilst you can get a career job on a cruise ship, the vast majority and the easier-to-get jobs, which I focus on here, are the contract jobs.

Secondly, crew divide into 'officers' and 'ratings'. This also applies to 'civilian' non-merchant marine crew and you'll probably find your job has either an 'officer' or a 'rating' status. So, just as the ship's captain is an officer and a deckhand is a rating, a shop assistant would be a rating, but a photographer, DJ or entertainer will probably hold officer status.

In practical terms, of course, all it means is that officers may use the ship's facilities and mix with the passengers (plus, perhaps, have a cabin with a porthole!). As a civilian non-mariner it won't make any difference to your work.

This 'family tree' gives a rough idea of how everyone works together :

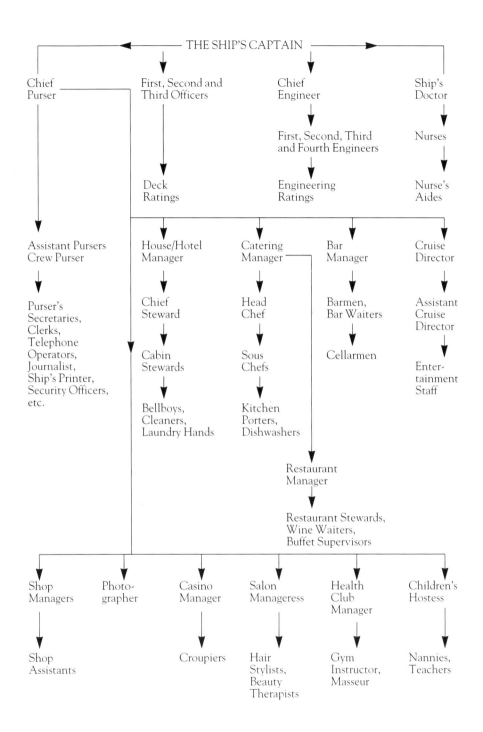

THE DEPARTMENTS

(Who Does What, Where and When!)

Just as in any large company, the running of a cruise ship is divided up into departments. Again, there's a definite hierarchy of crew within each department, all working in their own shipboard world, and often regarding the other departments either as rivals, or even deadly enemies!

Some of the departments are crewed mostly by career staff, others mostly by contract staff. The actual number of staff in each department, and the frequency with which vacancies arise, varies quite considerably. Here are the main departments you'll find on most ships :

The Deck Department

The Deck Department has direct responsibility for navigating and sailing the ship, plus overall responsibility for every related activity. That is, everything that is not the responsibility of the Engineering Department which, on most ships, is a world of its own!

The Deck Department is headed by the ship's Captain and most of the merchant marine officers are below him, running down through a very strict hierarchy to the deckhands.

The Engineering Department

As the name suggests, the Engineering Department is responsible for all engineering. At its most important, this includes running the ship's engines (most commonly diesel nowadays although there are still some steam ships). However, the department also controls all the maintenance work on board. So if a passenger breaks a lavatory handle or complains about a blown light bulb, someone will be despatched from the Engineering Department to fix it.

The Engineering Department is always treated with great respect. In the hierarchy, the Chief Engineer comes second only to the Captain, although most of them consider themselves far more important and will always talk about 'their' ship!

The Purser's Department

The Purser's Department is the management and administration centre. They handle all aspects of running the ship that are not to do with sailing it, or engineering. So, for example, tasks like Customs and immigration procedures, personnel, banking and accounting etc. are all handled here.

The Chief Purser is one of the most powerful people on board and rules over both the passengers and the crew! On most lines, the Chief Purser has seniority over all the other department heads, except Deck, Engineering and the Doctor.

The Hotel Department
The Hotel Department is responsible for all the accommodation on board the ship. In a land-based hotel this would probably be the equivalent of the Housekeeping Department. Hotel Department staff clean and present the cabins (which many cruise lines very glamorously call 'staterooms') and public areas and handle associated tasks, such as luggage and laundry. They do the same for the officers (everyone else has to DIY!).

The job of Cabin Steward/ess is one of the most numerous on any ship. It's also one of the jobs with the greatest number of vacancies.

The Catering Department
If you can eat it, the Catering Department controls it - ordering, preparing, cooking and serving. As cruise ships serve enormous quantities of high quality food, this is one of the biggest and most labour-hungry departments. On a typical ship you'll have a 500 seater restaurant plus several cafes and snack bars etc., serving seven meals a day -plus catering for the crew. The Catering Department also has a high turnover of staff.

The Bar Department
On the vast majority of cruise ships, the Bar Department is separate from the Catering Department. This is because it is a money-earning department (whereas most food is served free). A typical ship will operate a restaurant, nightclub and/ or disco, casino, several lounges and bars and provide bar service to the cabins, deck and poolside lido areas, plus a crew bar - serving an average of 11,000 drinks per day! Most jobs in this department are open to newcomers, with bar-tending staff liable to stay longer than bar waiters and waitresses.

The Cruise Department
(Also Known as the Social Department)

The Cruise Department is one of the most exciting departments on the ship. It is involved with every aspect of looking after and entertaining the passengers and making sure they enjoy their cruise. Many of the activities of the Cruise

Department are high profile - such as organising big-name cabaret shows, dances, parties or shore excursions for 500 passengers. Others are more personal, such as organising bridge classes or befriending lone passengers.

Jobs in this department are some of the most sought after on the ship and most of them are jobs that can simply be transferred from dry land. Working here is also the closest you'll ever get to being paid to go on a cruise!

The Special Departments

On every ship there are a number of special departments which don't come within any of the main departments (although overall responsibility for them usually rests with the Purser's Department). Some of these are controlled by the cruise line, but many are concessions. For the would-be crew member, the main advantage is that the jobs available are mostly land-based jobs which just happen to be done at sea!

The usual special departments are :

- Medical Services.
- Retail Outlets (such as the duty free shop, gift shop or boutique).
- Photography.
- The Casino.
- The Hair and Beauty Salons.
- The Health Club (gym, sauna, massage etc.).
- The Nursery.

THE JOBS

In this section, we'll go through all the many jobs that are available on board most ships. Actual job titles can vary according to the nationality of the ship in question, so do allow for this when making your applications.

The Deck Department

OFFICERS :

Captain	Chief Officer or First Officer
Second Officer	Third Officer

RATINGS :

Bosun	Deckhand

All the jobs in the Deck Department are for merchant mariners only and require special training and professional qualifications. Details of these are available from :

The College of Maritime Studies, Southampton Institute of Higher Education, Warsash Campus, Warsash, Southampton. SO3 6ZL. Telephone: 01489 576161 (Officers)

National Sea Training College, Denton, Gravesend, Kent. DA12 2HR. Telephone: 01474 363656 (Ratings)

The Co-Ordinating Agent, MNOT, 2-5 Minories, London E3 1BJ

The Engineering Department
OFFICERS :
Chief Engineer
Second Engineer
Third Engineer
Fourth Engineer

RATINGS :
Petty Officer Motorman
Motorman 1
Motorman 2

Many of the jobs in the Engineering Department are career jobs for merchant mariners and require appropriate training and professional qualifications. Details of these are available from :

The College of Maritime Studies, Southampton Institute of Higher Education, Warsash Campus, Warsash, Southampton. SO3 6ZL. Tel: 01489 576161 (Officers)

National Sea Training College, Denton, Gravesend, Kent. DA12 2HR. Tel: 01474 363656 (Ratings)

Ship Safe Training Group, 11-13 Canal Road, Rochester, ME2 4DS

However, there are contract jobs available for :

Maintenance Personnel
In most cases, the work involved is just the same as similar positions on dry land

and away from the engine room. The positions include :

CARPENTER, having experience of repair and maintenance.

ELECTRICIAN, with knowledge of commercial and industrial installations.

PLUMBER, with knowledge of commercial and industrial installations.

PAINTER and PAINTER/DECORATOR

MAINTENANCE ENGINEER/FITTER, with knowledge of a relevant area such as heating and ventilation, air conditioning, refrigeration, domestic and/or industrial appliances etc. Some ships even carry a fruit machine engineer or a TV repair engineer.

Some cruise ships employ CARPET FITTERS, TILERS etc. too! So it is always worth writing to see if your trade can be employed.

Engineering Department jobs are rarely advertised and so are best obtained by applying direct to the cruise lines. Alternatively, a few lines do employ sub-contractors for this work, in which case, application should be made to them (ask the cruise line for details).

You will need a relevant trade qualification (such as City & Guilds or NVQ's) and experience on land. This must be provable (i.e. you should have references). The preferred age range is 22-40, but not fixed. Rates of pay are similar to land-based jobs and all positions are of rating status.

The Purser's Department
CHIEF PURSER
Also Known As : The Hotel Manager

The Chief Purser is one of the most powerful people on board ship, with both passenger and crew responsibilities. Traditionally the Chief Purser was a merchant mariner. Some lines have now 'civilianised' the job and call the Purser a Hotel Manager, in which case the job should not be confused with that of House Manager in the Hotel Department!

The Chief Purser is the ship's business and administration manager. Duties include:

- Crew and passenger accounts.
- Payroll processing.
- Information distribution and internal communications.
- Purchasing.
- Personnel management.
- Management of concessions.
- Customs and Immigration matters.
- Reception duties and dealing with enquiries and complaints.

Many Chief Pursers are promoted from the ranks of Assistant Pursers, but those with experience can transfer from a land-based job. Application should be made direct to cruise lines. You will need three years 4/5 star hotel experience and a trade qualification, such as BTEC HND in Hotel & Catering or the HCIMA certificate.

Pay is US$60,000 per year on average and the job carries full officer status.

ASSISTANT PURSER
Also : Assistant Hotel Manager

On a large crew ship, there may be eight or ten Assistant Pursers. Firstly, they act as duty managers on a rota basis, standing in for the Chief Purser as necessary. However, Assistant Pursers also assume responsibility for a particular part of the Purser's Department function (see list above).

By and large, Assistant Pursers are not career mariners but are drawn from similar land-based jobs. You'll need at least two years of experience in one of the following fields : banking, hotel, restaurant, personnel, customer services, retail management or PA/secretary. A hotel and catering qualification helps, but is not always essential. Minimum age is often 25.

As Assistant Purser jobs are rarely advertised, you should write direct to cruise lines. Pay averages US$40,000 per year.

CREW PURSER

The Crew Purser is technically a personnel officer, although the job involves slightly more than personnel management and covers work rosters, crew pay and bonuses, as well as discipline, problems and complaints.

Applicants for Crew Purser should have several years of experience in the personnel department of a large company, a degree in personnel management, and be members of the Institute of Personnel Management. Application should be made direct to cruise lines. Not every ship will have a Crew Purser.

The position is salaried and carries officer status.

SECRETARY

The Purser's Office needs efficient secretarial support and this is provided by two or three secretaries who do a land-based job which just happens to be on a ship. This includes handling typing, reception work and acting as PA to the ship's officers.

Minimum requirements are one year's office experience and a typing speed of around 80 wpm. Knowledge of wordprocessing (such as WordPerfect) is desirable. Application should be made direct to cruise lines or, on occasion, to the Chief Purser.

Secretaries receive a salary and hold rating status. They are some of the few crew working normal office hours.

CASHIER

The Cashier (between 1-6 per ship) carries much responsibility in the Purser's Department and the work involves handling the finances for the ship, passengers and crew, including :

- Providing a banking service to the ship's bars and shops.
- Handling passenger accounts.
- Handling crew accounts.
- Providing Bureau de Change services.
- Paying bills.

Would-be cashiers should have at least three years' land-based cash-handling experience in a bank, building society, post office, accounts office or similar. Knowledge of computerised accounts is desirable. Apply direct to the cruise line or the Chief Purser.

These positions are salaried, with rating status. Some ships may employ a CHIEF CASHIER, requiring a minimum of five years' experience.

TELEPHONE OPERATOR

Modern telecommunications have reduced the demand for telephone operators. But, each cruise ship will need four or five to provide a 24 hour service. Work includes manning the internal switchboard together with placing and receiving satellite telephone calls, telexes, faxes and telegrams for passengers, crew, and ship's departments.

Applicants must be BT-trained or equivalent with sound experience in an international hotel or busy office. Fluency in a second language (French, German, Spanish or Japanese) is desirable but not essential.

Salaried position. Rating status.

CLERK

As in any office there is a considerable amount of administrative work to be done in the Purser's Department and other offices around the ship. Computerised systems have reduced the demand for clerks, but there is still some demand. The work is very much as in any land-based office.

Applicants must have at least two years' office experience. Experience in warehouse, stock control or purchasing is an advantage. Minimum age usually 19. You must have 4-5 good GCSE's including English Language and Maths. Apply direct to cruise lines or Chief Purser of ships.

Salaried job with rating status. Clerks work mostly office hours only.

POST OFFICE CLERK

Every ship has a post office for company, crew and passenger mail (in and out) and this is usually a duplicate of the postal system in the ship's country of registry. (For example, if you sail on a Norwegian ship out of Miami, you'll be licking Norwegian stamps for your letters home!) Three or four clerks are employed on each ship.

Applicants should have experience in a land-based post office, sorting office or mail room.

Salaried position, rating status.

RECEPTIONIST
Also : Information Officer/Concierge

An important role of the Purser's Department is passenger service and relations. Every ship has a hotel-style reception desk where passengers are checked in, checked out, and have their queries answered or their complaints tactfully received.

Would-be receptionists must have sound experience in customer services. Experience in a 4/5 star hotel is ideal, but those with experience in retail, banking or commerce may also be considered. Fluency in a second language (French, German, Spanish, Japanese) is desirable but not essential. Applicants must be of good appearance and well-mannered. Minimum age 21 for most cruise lines.

Apply direct to cruise lines or the Chief Purser.

Salaried position, rating status. Receptionists work round-the-clock and receive very little time off in port, which is their busiest period.

JOURNALIST

Most cruise ships run their own bulletin or newspaper. This brings passengers up to date with details of events, entertainments, ports of call, tours, the ship's facilities, and a digest of world news. Ships have between one and four journalists to write and publish this.

Ocean-going journalists should be aged 22-35 with all-round experience on a national, provincial or local newspaper, or be advertising copywriters. Knowledge of sub-editing or desk top publishing is useful.

The ship's journalists hold a salaried position but also often enjoy officer privileges.

PRINTER

The ship's printers (2-3 on a large ship) are responsible for printing the ship's newspaper (see above), promotional flyers (all of which are distributed to the cabins daily) and all the ship's internal memos and stationery.

Applicants require knowledge of offset Litho printing machinery, together with knowledge of basic maintenance for same. Apply direct to cruise lines, but note that vacancies are only occasional.

Salaried position, rating status.

SECURITY OFFICER

A number of ships, but by no means all, are now employing security guards. Their duties include both combating the threats of terrorism and piracy, theft, fraud and embezzlement, together with general security for passengers and crew.

Security officers should be aged 25-45 with a police, armed forces or private security background. There are both uniformed and plain clothes positions. Applications can be made direct to cruise lines and the private security services who provide this service as contractors (the individual cruise lines will advise).

Salaried position. Either rating or officer status depending on seniority.

Notes:

Notes:

THE HOTEL DEPARTMENT

HOUSE/HOTEL MANAGER

The Hotel Department is headed by the Hotel Manager (or, on ships with a Chief Purser, the House Manager). The House Manager's duties are, principally :

- Personnel management of Hotel Department staff, including work teams and rosters. - Stock ordering and control (including laundry). - Supervising presentation of cabins. - Supervising cleaning of public areas. - Dealing with problems and complaints.

House Managers should have at least five years' experience in a 4/5 star hotel, as either Hotel Manager or Assistant Manager. A professional qualification in hotel keeping is desirable (BTEC HND or similar), together with sound personnel management skills. Applications should be made direct to cruise lines. Such jobs are never usually advertised.

Salaried position, officer status.

CHIEF STEWARD

Also : Chief Cabin Steward

The Chief Cabin Steward is the House Manager's right hand man or woman and assists with the duties outlined above. In addition, the Chief Cabin Steward may personally provide cabin services to the Captain, senior officers and/or important passengers.

Chief Cabin Stewards are most usually recruited from the ranks of the Cabin Stewards, however, the position may also be filled by those with waiting experience gained in a good quality hotel or restaurant. Minimum age 25-30. A spoken knowledge of a second language is desirable but not essential.

Salaried position, rating status. A good Chief Cabin Steward might expect his or her tips to double his basic wage of US$20,000 per year.

CABIN STEWARD

The Cabin Stewards are responsible for cleaning and presentation of the passenger cabins (or staterooms as they are often known). A Cabin Steward's job extends much further than cleaning - A good Steward will provide his passenger with room service, deliver messages, run errands and generally carry out any special favour requested, such as arranging a basket of fruit at midnight or securing favoured places at the dinner table!

A few cruise lines have done away with these frills and merely employ Chambermaids. In both cases, both men and women are employed. A ship will have at least 80 Cabin Stewards, usually working in pairs and responsible for 15-20 cabins between them.

Applicants should have some experience in a good hotel or restaurant. Two years' experience is required by the better cruise lines. The minimum age is 22, and you should be of good appearance, polite and have a service orientated manner. Experience in providing hotel room service is an advantage.

Cabin Steward vacancies are regularly advertised by many of the cruise lines and their employment agencies. Most lines are also pleased to receive direct applications from suitable people.

Cabin Stewards receive a small basic salary plus tips (which are often guaranteed). Average total earnings are US$24,000 per year. The jobs hold rating status.

BELLBOY

All cruise lines employ bellboys in small numbers, as in any luxury hotel. Duties include luggage distribution, porterage, doorkeeping, lift attendant, and generally helping passengers.

Would-be bellboys should be of good appearance and hold 4-5 GCSE qualifications. They should have received training in a busy hotel. Applications should be made direct to cruise lines as such positions are rarely advertised.

Bellboys receive a basic salary plus tips at the discretion of passengers (no suggested minimum). Rating status.

CLEANER

The ship's Cleaners fulfil an essential role but have much less prestige than the Cabin Stewards, although their duties are very often the same. Usually, the cleaners are charged with the upkeep of all the public areas including corridors, foyers, the restaurant, disco, casino, and poolside lido areas. Although providing a 24-hour service, much of their work is undertaken between 12 midnight-7am. The cleaners also clean the galleys, officers' accommodation and communal areas in the staff quarters.

Applicants must have sound experience in using modern cleaning equipment in an environment requiring a high standard of finish - such as a top hotel, restaurant, prestigious office or retail location. Minimum preferred age 20, but not fixed.

Cleaner vacancies are regularly advertised by many of the cruise lines and their employment agencies. Most lines are also pleased to receive direct applications from suitable people. Some lines are considering awarding this work to sub-contractors.

Salaried position, no tips, with rating status.

LAUNDRY HAND

The ship's laundry is one of the most important areas of the ship, also one of the busiest on board and hardest working. Most laundries work 24 hours and employ 30 or 40 staff. On some ships, laundries are traditionally run by particular ethnic groups, such as the Chinese. The work involves providing a wet and dry cleaning laundry service for bedlinen, tableware and crew uniforms, together with a charged-for laundry service for crew and passengers.

Applicants must have experience in a commercial laundry, or a hotel or institutional laundry. Enquiries should be made with the cruise lines as to the availability of vacancies with them.

Salaried position, rating status. A productivity bonus or share of the charged-for laundry receipts may be paid.

The Catering Department
CATERING MANAGER

The Catering Manager is in overall control of all food preparation and service on board. His or her duties include :

- Overall control of restaurants, buffets and snack bars. - Personnel management. - Ordering and provisioning. - Costing and budgeting. - Menu planning (in conjunction with the Head Chef). - Planning of functions and parties. - Crew catering.

The Catering Manager is immediately superior to the Head Chef - who runs the galley -and the Maitre D - who runs the restaurant.

Intending catering managers must have at least five years' experience in a first class hotel or restaurant. Occasionally, those with good institutional catering experience may be accepted, together with experienced chefs and restaurant managers. A professional catering qualification is preferred.

Such jobs are rarely advertised. Direct application is the only way of securing a post.

Salaried position, with officer status.

Most cruise lines also require ASSISTANT CATERING MANAGERS, having 1-2 years' similar experience.

HEAD CHEF

The Head Chef is usually one of the larger than life characters on board. Like the Chief Engineer, he probably considers himself superior to the Captain! In actual fact, he'll spend very little time amongst his saucepans. Apart from lending his inspiration to the menus, the shipboard Head Chef is an administrator, personnel officer and quality controller as much as anything else.

Applicants must have five years' experience in 4/5 star hotel or restaurant and, preferably, a formal qualification.

Applications should be made direct to cruise lines. Few jobs of this nature are ever advertised.

Salaried position, officer status. (Few Head Chefs ever lower themselves by mingling with the passengers!)

On a large ship the Head Chef will often be aided by several ASSISTANT HEAD CHEFS OR FIRST CHEFS/COOKS, with similar experience but of 2-3 years minimum.

OTHER CHEFS

On an average ship there are likely to be at least 20 other chefs, each allocated to a particular function within the galley. Most of the jobs can be transferred directly from dry land and include:

- SENIOR SOUS CHEF.
- JUNIOR SOUS CHEF.
- SOUS CHEF.
- CHEF DE PARTIE.
- DEMI CHEF.
- BUTCHERS.
- COMMIS CHEF.
- BAKERS.

Applicants must have good experience in a first class hotel or restaurant or good institutional catering background. Two years is a preferred minimum, but not fixed. A trade qualification, such as City & Guilds 706/1 and 706/2 or equivalent NVQ's, very much preferred. Minimum age 25 (20 for a commis/junior chef).

Vacancies are advertised from time to time by the cruise lines, and their employment agencies. Most cruise lines will also consider direct applications at any time from suitable people.

Salaried position, rating status.

MAÎTRE D
Also : Restaurant Manager

The Maître d'Hotel is essentially a Restaurant Manager but the French term is in use, especially on ships operating from the USA. Although seemingly a minor role, it carries great seniority and ranks in status with the Head Chef (the pair are usually constantly at war!). The average cruise ship will hold a 500 seater restaurant which serves up to seven meals per day (two sittings for dinner). The

Maître D must organize sittings and seat plans which keep every passenger happy, and provide the superb service of a small restaurant on a school-canteen type scale!

Intending Maître D's should have at least five years' experience in a good hotel or restaurant. Those with experience as head waiter may be considered. A foreign language (French, German, Italian) is preferred but not essential. Minimum age usually 25.

Applications should be made direct to cruise lines. Few vacancies are ever advertised.

The Maître D earns a basic salary, plus tips. A top one can earn US$60,000 per year, making him or her one of the best paid crew members on board.

Many cruise lines employ ASSISTANT RESTAURANT MANAGERS requiring similar experience but of only 1-2 years.

RESTAURANT STEWARD
Also : Waiter

A great deal of importance is placed on the job of Restaurant Steward since good food and good service combined is one of the best ways to keep the passengers happy. The job is considered much, much harder than even the busiest hotel or restaurant!

A typical cruise ship will have 80 Restaurant Stewards. Typically they work in pairs. Some lines pair a Waiter and a Commis Waiter (Junior Waiter), others a Waiter and a Busboy (who fetches and carries). Even today, there are still very few females in the restaurant team. Restaurant Stewards who work together are often allocated to the same cabin!

Restaurant Stewards are hired in greater numbers and more frequently than almost any other shipboard profession, thus making it a 'way in' well worth considering for all newcomers.

Restaurant Stewards must have experience in a good quality hotel or restaurant and City & Guilds 700/1 and 700/3 qualifications (or NVQ's) are preferred. They should have a good knowledge of first class table service, preferably but not necessarily silver service. Spoken knowledge of another language (French, German, Italian) is an asset. Minimum age is usually 22 (19 for a Commis Waiter or Busboy). Maximum age to start usually 35, but flexible.

Jobs are advertised from time to time by most cruise lines or their agencies. Most will also welcome direct applications at any time from suitable people.

Restaurant Stewards receive a small basic salary (from US$500 per month) but, with tips, can make US$2,000 or more. Rating status.

Some cruise lines employ HEAD RESTAURANT STEWARDS OR HEAD WAITERS, similar experience but minimum 2-3 years.

WINE WAITER

Also : Sommelier

Most ships require between five and ten Wine Waiters, who recommend, take orders for, serve and supervise the wine in the ship's extensive cellars. As such, applicants must have a thorough knowledge of food and wine, preferably have undertaken a wine appreciation course, and have experience in a hotel or restaurant. Experience in a good quality wine bar or pub is acceptable to some cruise lines.

Foreign language knowledge (especially French) is an asset. The preferred age range is 28-45.

Vacancies are advertised from time to time by cruise lines and their agents, and most lines will welcome direct applications at any time from suitable people.

A Wine Waiter receives a modest basic salary plus commission on wine sold. He may also receive tips, but the amount is not fixed. Rating status.

BUFFET SUPERVISOR

Buffets are a feature of every cruise. These are available at most times of the day -breakfast, brunch, lunch, afternoon tea - even a midnight buffet! Buffet Supervisors organize and present these lavish and extensive displays.

Applicants should have experience in a good hotel or restaurant. In particular, they should have experience in carvery, flambe dishes, barkeeping and be able to supervise Restaurant Stewards. Minimum age is usually 22. As only a small number of vacancies arise, they are rarely advertised. Applications should be made direct to cruise lines.

Salaried position, possible tips. Rating status.

MEALS SERVED
ON A TYPICAL CRUISE SHIP

6.30am - 9.30am
Breakfast, served to passengers in their cabins.

7.30am - 10.00am
Full breakfast served in the restaurant.

10.30am - 11.30am
Coffee and pastries, served in one of the lounges, and/or brunch, served in the buffet.

12 noon - 2.30pm
Lunch served in the restaurant, together with an extensive buffet/ smorgasbord served in the poolside lido.

4.00pm - 5.30pm
Afternoon tea, served in the lounges, or brought to the cabins.

4.30pm - 5.30pm
Early tea for children, served in the restaurant.

6.00pm - 8.00pm
Various cocktail parties, held in the various lounges and bars including, on the first night of every cruise, the Captain's Cocktail Party.

7.00pm - 8.30pm
First sitting for dinner, served in the restaurant.

8.30pm - 10.00pm
Second sitting for dinner, served in the restaurant.

12 midnight - 1.00am
The midnight buffet. A traditional feature of almost every cruise is a lavish buffet supper served at midnight!

KITCHEN PORTER
Also : Galley Hand

A Kitchen Porter has one of the lowliest jobs on the ship, and one of the hardest! It involves storekeeping, portering, basic food preparation (e.g.. peeling) and cleaning. On a typical cruise ship there will be 45 Kitchen Porters.

Despite the low status, applicants should not be complete newcomers, but SHOULD have some provable experience of working in a busy hotel, restaurant, institutional or commercial kitchen. Vacancies are advertised by cruise lines and agencies from time to time and applications should also be made direct.

Salaried position, rating status.

DISHWASHER

Dishwashing is not necessarily the job it might seem. Modern cruise ships make extensive use of dishwashing machinery rather than Brillo pads! However, applicants should have some experience in a hotel, restaurant, institutional or commercial kitchen -if not necessarily in dishwashing, then in cleaning or portering. Applications should be made direct to cruise lines.

Salaried position, rating status.

The Bar Department

BAR MANAGER

The Bar Manager undertakes a very similar job to that in a pub or hotel bar - but on a much larger scale. Apart from bar service to a 500 seater restaurant, the average ship will have around ten bars; including the lounges, casino, nightclub, poolside lido, room service and crew bar. The Bar Manager has overall control of ordering, stock, personnel, cash, accounting and Customs procedures. It is a senior position, not coming under the control of the Catering Manager.

Bar Managers must have at least five years' management experience in a busy bar environment, such as a hotel, restaurant, club, leisure centre etc. Minimum age 25-30 at least.

As such jobs are never advertised, applications must be made direct to cruise lines.

Salaried position, officer status. Usually no tips or commission.

Also required are ASSISTANT BAR MANAGERS (6-8 per ship). At least one year's experience. Some lines MAY accept those with good pub experience as a Bar Manager or Head Barman.

BARMAN
Also : Bartender

The American term Bartender is taken by many cruise lines. A typical ship will have 20-30 Barmen (very few women are taken on for this position). Generally, the job is much more demanding than in a pub and includes serving drinks direct to passengers. Bar Waiters (see below) are also responsible for stock, accounting (most lines offer passengers a charge account for bar purchases), cash, and bar presentation.

Barmen must have experience in a 4/5 star hotel or good restaurant. In particular, they must have a thorough knowledge of cocktails. Knowledge of a second language and an IBA or City & Guilds qualification or similar is desirable. Minimum age 22.

Vacancies are advertised from time to time by cruise lines and their agencies. Applications should also be made direct.

Salaried position, rating status. Barmen also receive a commission on sales (from 1.5%) and can expect (but are not guaranteed) tips, plus free drinks (which they must usually take as a tip!).

Also required are HEAD BARMEN. As above but minimum two years' experience (five preferred) and must have a relevant qualification.

BAR WAITER
Also : Bar Steward or Cocktail Waiter

An average cruise ship will have 40 or more Bar Waiters who man the various lounges, nightclub, casino, poolside lido etc. Unlike a Barman, this job is equally open to women.

Applicants must have experience in a good quality hotel, restaurant or nightclub. They must have a knowledge of wine, cocktails and non-alcoholic beverages. An IBA qualification is an advantage. Minimum age 19 (sometimes 22). Bar waiters must also be of good appearance and with a pleasant personality.

Vacancies are advertised from time to time by cruise lines and their agencies. Most cruise lines will also consider direct applications at any time from suitable people.

Small basic salary. Rating status. Bar Waiters can expect tips (often guaranteed by way of a service charge levied on bills) and may also receive a commission on sales.

CELLARMAN

The work is very much like that in a pub, hotel or nightclub. (Is there a cellar on a ship?!) Applicants must have good experience of cellarwork (preferably in a 4/5 star hotel), including a working knowledge of fine wines, stock ordering, accounting and keeping. A knowledge of Customs and duty free procedures would be an advantage.

Apply direct to the cruise line, or the Bar Manager.

Salaried position, rating status.

The Cruise Department
(Or Social Department)
CRUISE DIRECTOR

Cruise Director is one of the most exciting jobs on any ship! The Cruise Director is responsible for ensuring passengers have a good time. This includes conceiving, organising and running daily entertainment such as cabarets, shows, sporting activities, shore excursions, parties, classes, lectures and much more besides.

Would-be Cruise Directors should have a hotel, leisure, theatre, sporting or tour operating background, with a really **buzzing** personality, and have some management experience. Some (but not all) cruise lines will consider those with experience in a holiday camp, leisure centre, or as a travel courier or PR host/hostess in a hotel or nightclub etc.

These jobs are rarely advertised and mostly found by direct application to cruise lines.

Cruise Directors are paid a basic salary and hold senior officer status. They don't receive tips but should never need to buy a drink for themselves!

ASSISTANT CRUISE DIRECTOR

Assistant Cruise Directors assist the Cruise Director with the ship's entertainment programme. There will be 10-12 on a large ship. Apart from helping out overall, you will usually be responsible for a particular activity - for example, you might be put in charge of deck sports, activities for children, or single passengers.

No specific experience is demanded for Assistants, but they must have a pleasant personality and, for a fun cruise line, be extremely lively and outgoing. Experience of working in a hotel, nightclub, leisure centre, fun pub, holiday camp etc. would be useful. Preferred ages 22-35. As Assistants are often required to participate in cabarets or shows, some talent in this area (as an amateur singer, musician etc.) would help!

Such jobs are rarely, if ever, advertised. Those interested must write direct to cruise lines and convince them! Competition for this job is pretty fierce.

Assistant Cruise Directors earn a salary and hold officer status. (This is the nearest to free cruising that you will ever get!)

Some cruise lines also employ HOSTS/HOSTESSES to present and/or 'mingle' at functions. Basic requirements are as above, but less experience is needed and it is unnecessary to be able to sing or dance! If you are an amiable person, easy to get on with and have a friendly disposition ... this position could be for you. Why not try!

TRAVEL AGENT

The ship's travel agents devise, organise, sell and conduct shore excursions. This might include an afternoon coach or walking tour in Jamaica, or an air excursion to Aztec ruins in Mexico. The travel agents also make onward travel arrangements for departing passengers and crew.

Applicants must have a minimum of two years' experience in a travel agency environment, and a minimum professional qualification, such as COTAC or the NVQ's in Travel Skills.

Vacancies are rarely advertised and applications should be made direct to cruise lines. Travel agents receive a basic salary plus bonus/commission on sales. Some lines allow use of the ship's facilities, mainly so that they can mix and promote their services!

Also required are TOUR GUIDES to conduct shore excursions. You should have tour guide or rep./courier experience either at home or abroad and ideally a 'blue badge' issued by your local tourist board. A second language is useful. Salary plus tips.

ENTERTAINERS AND OTHER CRUISE DEPARTMENT STAFF

Modern cruising is all about entertainment, hence a wide range of entertainers are needed to provide passengers with a non-stop programme. Good semi-professional entertainers may have the chance to work alongside the big stars. Some of the lines operating several ships in the Caribbean fly their entertainers from ship to ship by helicopter for nightly shows.

Some of the jobs available include :

SINGER, soloist, duet or group. Any age.

DANCERS, all types (including 'exotic'!).

MC (Master of Ceremonies), to present cabarets and shows.

DJ (2-4 per ship), for the disco, nightclub and parties. Age 24-34 preferred.

MAGICIAN/CONJURER/ILLUSIONIST, and similar acts.

CHILDREN'S ENTERTAINER, to present shows, magic tricks, parties and help with special activities.

CHILDREN'S HOST/YOUTH COUNSELLOR, to conduct programmes for 5-17's. Preferably to have two years' experience with children.

DANCE TEACHER, must be highly skilled in all types, including sequence, old time and/or disco. Couples accepted.

MUSICIANS, solo or band, all types.

PIANIST/ORGANIST, with cocktail bar or concert experience.

COMEDIAN. Depending on the type of cruises offered. Some club experience usually essential.

BRIDGE, CHESS, CARDS INSTRUCTOR etc. Must play to a good standard and, preferably, have coaching experience.

LIBRARIAN, for ships with a library; previous experience of working in a library usually required.

FILM PROJECTIONIST, for the ship's cinema. Previous experience essential.

TV PRODUCER. A small number of ships have shipboard closed circuit TV for passengers and crew and offer entertainment and information stations.

VIDEO CAMERAMAN, to film parties and functions. Experience working in a production studio or similar usually required.

RADIO DJ. Most ships have several closed circuit radio channels. Must have hospital/campus radio experience minimum. Note: If you have a good voice and are interested in radio, most hospital radio stations will be pleased to hear from you - this could be another easy route into working on board cruise ships.

LECTURER/HOBBY TEACHER. Many cruise lines employ specialists to, for example, give foreign language lessons or lecture on the history of the areas being visited.

SPORTS INSTRUCTOR. A very important aspect of most cruises nowadays. Instructors are required in many fields, especially GOLF, TENNIS, SQUASH, SCUBA DIVING, SNORKELLING, WATER SKIING, WIND SURFING, CLAY PIGEON SHOOTING, FISHING etc. Must be qualified and have one year's experience in coaching.

Note: If you're involved in any sort of sport/entertainment it's worth offering your services. If that entertainment doesn't currently exist, many lines may consider introducing it. In addition, theme cruises are becoming very popular and need suitable instructors/lecturers. For example, Canberra hosts bird watching, football, jazz and photography theme cruises!

All entertainers must be experienced in hotels, clubs or at social functions. You do not have to be a professional entertainer - amateurs are accepted by the cruise lines, but the standard required will depend on the cruise line in question.

SAMPLE ENTERTAINMENT PROGRAMME FOR A SMALL CRUISE SHIP

7.30am
Ship's radio station opens. Music, world news and 'what's on'.

8.00am
Early morning 'keep fit' classes on deck.

9.30am
Kids' Club starts for the day, with a programme of games, activities and entertainment through until 8.30pm.
If in port, excursion coaches leave for today's excursions.

10.00am
Deck sports begin. Tennis, table tennis, football, cricket, golf driving, clay pigeon shooting. If at anchor, watersports and fishing.

12 noon
The ship's cinema opens, showing the latest releases until 1am.

1.30pm
Special interest talks, lectures and courses begin.

4.00pm
The traditional time for tea dances, plus quizzes, bingo, or a concert or show in the ship's theatre.

7.00pm
The ship's casino swings into business until 1am.

8.30pm/9.00pm
Evening entertainment in the main lounges - a cabaret, floor show, mini-musical, folklore show, theme evening, dancing etc.

10.00pm
The ship's disco or nightclub begins pumping out the hits until 1.30am or so.

Some jobs for entertainers are advertised or obtained through theatrical agents. 'The Stage' journal is the best source of both. Alternatively, apply direct to cruise lines. If appropriate, submit an audio or video cassette of your act.

Entertainers are paid a basic salary and, in some cases, a bonus for each performance. Entertainers have officer status and can use all the ship's facilities and mix with the passengers. They also often receive superior cabins! However, because of the need to vary the entertainment programme, they may only be offered short term contracts of 1-3 months.

The Special Departments

Medical Services

Every ship has a well equipped and staffed medical centre (sick bay) and many have an operating theatre. As well as providing routine and emergency treatment to the passengers this facility also acts as a local general practice for the crew.

DOCTOR

Every ship has at least one Doctor who is usually a qualified surgeon, plus one or two junior doctors who should have experience in general practice and/or accident and emergency. Some ships carry a DENTAL SURGEON and an experienced DENTAL NURSE.

NURSE

Every ship will carry at least two Nurses; in addition, some will have a SISTER or MATRON. Nurses must be qualified RGN's or equivalent, with minimum five years' experience in as many hospital departments as possible, including some accident and emergency and, preferably, theatre experience.

NURSE'S AIDE

Two or three required on a larger ship. Must be qualified SEN's or equivalent, with two years' experience in a hospital, general practice or nursing home.

All medical positions are obtained by direct application to the cruise lines. All positions are salary only and rating status (apart from the Doctors who live a life of prestige and luxury!).

Retail Outlets
(The Ship's Shops!)

The range of shopping facilities on board ship ranges from a few kiosks on a small ship, to full shopping arcades. The liner Norway has two grand ship-long malls named Fifth Avenue and Champs Elysees! Types of shop now on board many ships include a DUTY FREE SHOP, a GENERAL STORE, a PHARMACY, a CLOTHING BOUTIQUE, a GIFT SHOP, a PERFUMERY, and a JEWELLERS. The QE2 even has a FLORIST!

Applicants for these positions must have land-based experience in one of the types of shop on board. Experience in a good quality department store is much preferred. There are two types of position :

GIFT SHOP ASSOCIATE (GIFT SHOP ASSISTANT)

Should have minimum one year's experience in retailing, preferably two (experience in duty free sales is ideal) and be aged minimum 22, maximum 40. A second language (French, German, Spanish, Italian) is an asset but not essential. You should have a pleasing appearance and a pleasant personality.

GIFT SHOP MANAGER/ESS

Should have minimum five years' experience in retailing, either in a management or supervisory post. Minimum age usually 26.

Retail positions are advertised from time to time by the cruise lines, concessionaires and agencies, but those with experience should also approach potential employers direct. Note that most retail shops are now operated by concessionaires. The relevant cruise line should be able to provide details of these.

Retail shop staff receive a basic salary plus commission and/or bonus. Most cruise lines allow them access to the ship's facilities on a limited basis.

Photography
PHOTOGRAPHER

On every cruise ship the ship's photographers are ever-ready with their cameras - they snap the passengers on arrival, at the Captain's cocktail party, at dinner, on deck, on excursions and, on occasions, in their cabins (where they are not supposed to be!). These photographs are processed overnight and sold the next day in the photo shop (except the cabin ones of course!). A ship will have between one and four photographers. It's usual to have a chief photographer and one or more assistants (see below).

Applicants should be experienced professional photographers with a pleasant personality and not afraid to work hard (often all through the night). Experience of weddings and portrait photography will be a definite advantage. Other than that there are no special requirements. Application can be made direct to the cruise lines or, in most cases, one of the photographic concessionaires. Photographers hold officer status.

Photographers earn a basic salary and commission on sales. Most cruise lines allow them to mix with the passengers and use the ship's facilities.

Also required are PHOTOPROCESSING ASSISTANTS, with experience of automatic photoprocessing equipment, to process the photographer's pictures and offer a charged-for processing service to the passengers and crew. On some ships the photographers must also be able to do this.

The Casino
Most ships feature a casino (though not all) and in some, the casino is the centre of the cruise. Many Americans take 3-4 day 'casino cruises' to the Bahamas - to escape the ban on casinos in most US states. Most casinos are concessions and very important sources of income for the ship. British trained casino staff are considered the best in the world and make up the majority of the staff in most floating casinos. The jobs available are :

CASINO MANAGER & ASSISTANT MANAGERS
CASHIER
CROUPIER (Up to 50 on a large ship.)

Applicants must be trained, qualified and licensed croupiers with at least one year's experience in a land-based casino (preferably 18 months). Must have thorough knowledge of roulette and blackjack. Minimum age 21.

Applicants with suitable experience should apply, at any time, to one of the casino concessionaires, or the cruise lines direct. Those wishing to train as croupiers should seek a vacancy as a trainee by contacting land-based casinos in their region (see your telephone directory). The minimum age is 18. The inexperienced should not apply for any shipboard position.

Casino staff earn a basic salary and may receive 'chips as tips' (not guaranteed). Croupiers hold rating status.

The Hair and Beauty Salons

Every ship has a hairdressing salon, catering for both men and women. Many also have beauty salons which offer the full range of beauty treatments. On an average ship, up to 20 staff may be involved in providing these services and the work is basically the same as in any good quality land-based salon. The jobs available are :

SALON MANAGER/ESS
HAIR STYLIST
BEAUTY THERAPIST

Applicants should have experience in a good quality (preferably city-centre) hair or beauty salon, with extensive knowledge of traditional and modern styling and modern beauty products and processes. City & Guilds or National Vocational qualifications in Gents/Ladies Hairdressing or Beauty Therapy are helpful. Selection is usually by means of a trade test.

Application should generally be made to the concessionaires or agents - such as Steiner or Coiffeur Transocean. They can advise whether an applicant is likely to be suitable.

Hair and beauty staff earn a salary, tips and commission or bonus on products sold. Contracts are usually between four months and one year. Most lines allow staff limited access to the ship's facilities.

The Health Club

The Health Club has become one of the most popular facilities on every ship, and on the newer ships these are quite lavish, featuring several swimming pools, gyms, dance studios, saunas, Turkish baths and even squash and tennis courts!

A range of staff are needed as follows :

HEALTH CLUB MANAGER/ESS, with management or supervisory experience in a land-based health club or leisure centre. A BTEC National Diploma in Leisure or HND in Leisure Studies would be an advantage. Age 25-35.

GYM/FITNESS INSTRUCTOR, with minimum one year's experience and a professional qualification (YMCA minimum). Age 22+.

AEROBICS INSTRUCTOR, with minimum one year's experience and a teaching qualification. Age 22+.

MASSEUR AND MASSEUSE, with minimum two years' experience and a professional qualification. Age 25+.

SWIMMING POOL ATTENDANT, with Royal Life Saving Society Bronze award.

Health Club facilities are operated either by cruise lines directly or by concessionaires. Vacancies are advertised from time to time but suitable people should also apply direct.

Health Club staff receive a basic salary and may also receive commission or tips. Rating status for most jobs.

The Nursery

The extent of this department depends on the cruise line and ship - ie., whether it is one to attract many families or not. Canberra even has its own night nursery. On a family-orientated cruise line, the jobs available would include :

CHILDREN'S HOST, to have five years' experience working with children in a nursery, or be a qualified primary school teacher.

CRECHE ASSISTANT, to have at least one year's experience in a professional creche or nursery. Minimum age 20.

NANNY/BABYSITTER, to have one year's experience, and nannies to have a professional qualification, such as NNEB. Minimum age 20.

TUTOR/TEACHER. Required on some ships. Must be qualified, preferably Maths/English/Sciences/Humanities and with five years' experience in teaching 5-11's or 11-16's.

Application should be made direct to cruise lines. All positions are salaried and nannies/babysitters can expect to receive tips. Rating status.

Note : Unless otherwise stated, most of the jobs covered in this section are open to men and women, regardless of the job title. However, do note that not all cruise lines necessarily have equal opportunities policies and are not necessarily governed by the equal opportunities laws of any particular country.

CHECKLIST

Here's space to list your preferred choice of jobs :

First Choice :

Second Choice :

Third Choice :

Notes:

Chapter 7

DIRECTORY OF EMPLOYERS

Employer : Abercrombie & Kent
Description : Specialises in adventure cruising (such as, for example, whale-spotting) rather than traditional cruising. The ship carries 100 passengers and 100 crew.

Ships : *Explorer.*

Cruises : Mostly Antarctica.

Contact : 1520 Kensington Road, Oak Brook. IL60521. USA.

Employer : Airtours
Description : Brand new British cruise line owned by the Airtours holiday company and offering budget-priced fun cruising.

Ships : *Seawing, Carousel.*

Cruises : Mediterranean, Canary Isles.

Contact :

Entertainments Officers : Overseas Personnel, Wavell House, Holcombe Road, Helmshore, Rossendale. Lancs BB4 4NB

All Other Positions : V Ships (Agency), 'Aigue Marine', 24 Av. de Fontvieille, PO Box 639, MC98013. Monaco.

Employer : American Canadian Caribbean Line
Description : ACC mainly offers longer cruises (usually a minimum of two weeks) between the north-eastern ports of the USA (including New York) and the Caribbean.

Ships : *New Shoreham II, Caribbean Prince, Mayan Prince, Niagara.*

Cruises : Caribbean.

Contact : 461 Water Street, PO Box 368, Warren. RI02885. USA.

Employer : American Hawaii

Description : American Hawaii specialises in cruising around the Hawaiian Islands using two elegant 1950's cruise liners. The company's vessels (total capacity 1,550 passengers) are some of the only cruise liners registered in the USA. This can serve to restrict employment of foreign nationals. Foreigners are only likely to be employed if no US national is available to do the job in question.

Ships : *Constitution, Independence.*

Cruises : Mostly Hawaii only.

Contact : 550 Kearney Street, San Francisco. CA94108. USA.

Employer : Carnival Cruise Lines

Description : Carnival Cruise Lines is the leading 'fun' cruise line in the USA and all its cruises (mostly operating out of Miami to the Caribbean) offer a party atmosphere. Carnival does not offer traditional style cruising and there is no trace of stuffiness or formality aboard its vessels. As a result crew tend to be younger and, experience aside, a happy and cheerful personality is important. Carnival is one of the most successful cruise lines at the moment.

Carnival ships can carry a total of 15,000 passengers (served by 8,000 crew) between them. Carnival has recently stated that it will introduce four more ships within the next three years, so certainly a name to look out for!

Carnival have recently set up a subsidiary called Fiesta Marina Cruises. This company operates the Fiesta Marina to serve the South American market (crew for this ship should speak good Spanish).

Ships : *Ecstasy, Fantasy, Festivale, Holiday, Tropicale, Fiesta Marina, Celebration, Jubilee, Fascination, Imagination, Sensation.*

Cruises : Mostly Caribbean, Jubilee presently cruises from Los Angeles.

Contact : Randy Coldham, Recruitment Manager, Carnival Cruise Lines, Walter House, 418-422 Strand, London WC2R 0PT

(Applications should be made to Carnival's London office, rather than their US headquarters.)

Employer : Chandris Cruises
Chandris Celebrity and Chandris Fantasy

Description : Chandris is a long-established Greek shipping company whose distinctive blue funnel, bearing a white cross, is known worldwide. The 'Celebrity' brand name is more upmarket, and uses larger, newer and more luxurious ships demanding a higher standard of service. The 'Fantasy' brand name is more fun orientated. The company also operates tankers!

Most Chandris officers are Greek, but positions are open to all suitable applicants. Horizon and Zenith are almost identical in design and accommodate 1,374 passengers each.

Ships : *Britanis, Horizon, Meridian, Zenith, Amerikanis.*

Cruises : Worldwide, mostly in Caribbean and Mediterranean.

Contact :

5 St. Helen's Place, London EC3A 6BJ 5200 Blue Lagoon Drive, Miami. FL33126. USA. 95 Akti Miaouli, 18538 Piraeus. Athens. Greece.

Employer : Classical Cruise Line

Description : Small-scale cruise line operating special-interest cruises worldwide. Each ship carries only 80 passengers and lectures and talks are the main form of entertainment on board.

Ships : *Aurora I, Aurora II.*

Cruises : Worldwide.

Contact : 132 E. 70th Street, New York. NY10021. USA.

Employer : Clipper Cruise Line

Description : Operates cruises along the coast of the USA and in the Caribbean.

Ships : *Yorktown Clipper, Nantucket Clipper, World Discoverer.*

Cruises : In and around the USA.

Contact : 7711 Bonhomme Avenue, St. Louis. MO63105. USA.

Employer : Club Med.

Description : Offers relaxed cruising aboard its sail cruise ships. The atmosphere on board is similar to the Club Med. holiday villages. It is advisable to have a good knowledge of French for all jobs, although English is also spoken by most of the crew.

Ships : *Club Med. I, Club Med. II.*

Cruises : Caribbean, South Pacific.

Contact : 40 W. 57th Street, New York. NY10019. USA.

UK Representation : 106 Brompton Road, London SW3 1JJ

Employer : Color Line

Description : All their ships are registered as 'Roll on-Roll off' ferries. They operate up and down the Norwegian coast etc. Although some passengers do take their trips for pleasure, it is not a true cruise line. Laughably my competitors have listed this company as a cruise line in their so-called cruise ship 'guides'. However, it is no more a cruise line than the Dover-Calais ferry companies in England! If you do want to try them their address is :

Contact : B. Skaugen Shipping A/S, Haakon V11 Gaten 1, Box 1611, Vika N-0119, Oslo 1, Norway.

Employer : Commodore Cruise Line

Description : Commodore is a smaller cruise line, but has a long standing reputation amongst passengers. Currently the line operates just one ship. It has a higher proportion of European crew than some companies.

Ships : *Enchanted Seas.*

Cruises : Caribbean.

Contact : 800 Douglas Road, Suite 700, Coral Gables. FL33114. USA.

Employer : Compagnie Francaise de Croisières
(Croisières Pacquet)

Description : Pacquet is a famous and much respected traditional French cruise line, now also the last in this country. It has a reputation for traditional service and a very high standard of cuisine. All nationalities may apply for jobs but very good French must be spoken as the atmosphere on board is similar to a top class Paris hotel. Pacquet offers cultural theme cruises, including an annual Music Festival at Sea!

Ships : *Mermoz*.

Cruises : Worldwide, mostly Middle East, Indian Ocean, South America (one of the few ships to do so).

Contact :

Shops and Entertainment Staff : 5 Boulevard Malesherbes, 75008 Paris. France.

All Other Positions : Navigestion (Agency), Le Schuylkil, 19 Boulevard de Suisse, Monte Carlo 9800. Monaco.

Employer : Costa Cruises
Description : Costa, whose ships are marked with a very distinctive giant 'C' on the funnel, is a very well established Italian line with a long history. It has mostly Italian officers but an international crew with a reputation for style and traditional service. Recent additions to the fleet mean that all the Costa-named ships are currently less than four years old.

Ships : *Costa Allegra, Costa Classica, Costa Romantica, Costa Marina, Daphne.*

Cruises : Worldwide but mostly in the Mediterranean and Caribbean.

Contact : Via G D'annunzio, PO Box 389, Genoa. Italy. 1 Biscayne Tower, 100 South Biscayne Boulevard, Miami. FL33133. USA. UK Representation (not Personnel) : 10 Frederick Close, London W2 2HD

Employer : Crystal Cruises
Description : Crystal is now Japanese owned but serves the international market and offers a very exclusive (and expensive) style of cruising. Crew members are recruited internationally.

Ships : *Crystal Harmony, Crystal Symphony* (due to enter service).

Cruises : Caribbean, South America, occasionally Mediterranean.

Contact : 2121 Avenue of the Stars, Los Angeles. CA90067. USA.

Employer : CTC Cruise Lines

Description : CTC is Ukrainian/Russian owned and operated and sails western-built cruise ships carrying 550-750 passengers each. It is one of the few lines offering cruises originating in the UK, sailing from Tilbury, Liverpool, Bristol and Scotland as well as Southampton where most UK cruises depart.

CTC offers budget priced cruising. However, their cruise itineraries are some of the most innovative and include cruises to almost every part of the world including Australia and around Africa!

Although most staff are Ukrainian/Russian a large proportion of the passengers are British; entertainment and administrative staff (about 35 each ship) are hired in the UK.

Ships : *Kareliya, Azerbaydzhan, Gruziya, Southern Cross.*

Cruises : Worldwide.

Contact (UK Office): 1 Regent Street, London SW1Y 4NN

Employer : Cunard Line

Description : Cunard is one of the longest established and most famous cruise lines, operating the most famous liner, QE2. Cunard is much smaller than it was in the heyday of the ocean liners but still one of the biggest cruise lines in the world in terms of number of ships operated.

Cunard is considered by many as the last 'real' cruise line. QE2 is almost the last ship in the world to offer a regular, scheduled passenger transport service rather than package holiday cruises as most other lines do. This ship is also the most luxurious of all and, not unreasonably, one of the most expensive to sail on.

Cunard has one of the largest crew requirements, with a high proportion of British crew (1,000 on QE2 alone). Standards are very high and there is always much competition for jobs. Cunard employees tend to stay with the company.

Cunard currently has four operating styles :

QE2 : Operating the *Queen Elizabeth 2* offering luxury cruises on various itineraries around the world, including world cruises and scheduled transatlantic crossings.

Cunard Royal Viking : Operating *Royal Viking Sun, Sagafjord* and *Vistafjord, Sea Goddess I* and *Sea Goddess II*. These are super-luxury ships with extremely high standards and attracting the most discerning and wealthy passengers.

QE2 carries up to 1,766 passengers, *Royal Viking Sun* 740, *Sagafjord* 513, *Vistafjord* 677, and the smaller *Sea Goddess I* and *II*, 120 each.

Cunard Crown: Operating *Cunard Countess, Cunard Princess, Crown Jewel, Crown Dynasty* and *Crown Monarch*. These are slightly smaller than many of the vast ships sailing today. The idea is to offer more intimate cruising and access to smaller ports. *Cunard Crown* also has a more informal style. Each ship carries 800 passengers, except *Crown Monarch* which carries 530 passengers.

At present, *Cunard Countess* and *Crown Jewel* are based in the Caribbean, *Crown Dynasty* in the Caribbean/Mexico, US west coast and Alaska, *Cunard Princess* is in the Canary Islands/Mediterranean and *Crown Monarch* is in the South Pacific.

Cunard Crown now includes tips for restaurant and cabin staff in the price of its cruises.

River Cruising: European river cruising on the *Danube Princess, Prussian Princess, Princess de Provence, Dresden* and *Mozart*.

Contact :

Fleet Personnel, South Western House, Canute Road, Southampton SO14 3NR

For cruise department also: Cunard Line, Entertainment Dept., 555 5th Avenue, New York. NY10017. USA.

We also suggest you contact: Logbridge Ltd. (see Concessionaires/Agencies section in this book) for hotel/catering/bar department ratings.

Employer : DFDS

Description : A major Danish shipping company. Most of its fleet operate European ferry services but it operates one ferry-cum-cruise ship in the Caribbean.

Ships : *Hamburg*.

Cruises : Caribbean.

Contact : Sankt Anna Plads 30, DK-1295 Copenhagen K. Denmark.

Employer : Diamond Cruise
Description : A small Finnish-owned line offering high-quality cruising, but with a relaxed atmosphere. Has a large proportion of female staff. The Diamond is a twin-hull cruise ship. More ships are planned over the next few years.

Ships : *Radisson Diamond, Kungsholm* (due in service).

Cruises : Mediterranean (summer) and Caribbean (winter).

Contact : Concorde Centre, 2875 NE 191st. Street, Suite 304, North Miami Beach. FL33180. USA.

Employer : Discovery Cruises
Description : Operates a single ship on very short (some are just one day long!) cruises from Port Everglades, Florida, USA. Small crew requirement.

Ships : *Discovery I.*

Cruises : Florida coastal waters.

Contact : 1850 Eller Drive, Suite 402, Fort Lauderdale. FL33316. USA.

Employer : Dolphin Cruise Line
Description : Dolphin Cruise Line is owned by the same company as Majesty Cruise Line (see separate entry) with Dolphin being a more budget-conscious operation and Majesty a more upmarket line. Most officers are Greek but all other crew members are recruited internationally and number some 1,300.

Ships : *Oceanbreeze, Seabreeze, Dolphin IV.*

Cruises : Miami to the Bahamas only. Each cruise lasts no more than 3-4 days.

Contact : 901 South America Way, Miami. FL33132. USA.

Employer : Epirotiki Lines
Description : Epirotiki (pronounced Eh-peer-ah-tee-kee) is a long established and traditional Greek company which cruises in the Mediterranean (mostly the

Greek islands). It also operates under two other cruising names, Royal European and Mediterranean Cruises.

Officers are mainly Greek but all positions are open to suitable foreigners. Each of the vessels, which are mainly older, more traditional style ships, carry 150-200 crew.

Ships : *Appollo, Argonaut, Odysseus, Jason, Hermes, World Renaissance, Mistral, Olympic, Neptune, Orpheus, Pallas Athena, Triton.*

Cruises : Mediterranean and Aegean.

Contact : 87 Akti Miaouli, 18538 Piraeus, Athens. Greece.

Employer : Hapag Lloyd
Description : Hapag Lloyd is a major German cargo line and the group also includes an airline. However, it does operate a single ship (758 passengers) serving the German market.

Ships : *Europa.*

Cruises : Europe/Mediterranean.

Contact : Ballindamm, PO Box 102626, 2000 Hamburg 1. Germany.

Employer : Holland America Line
Description : Holland America is a long established cruise line. The company is known for extremely high standards of service and was also the first to offer theme cruises, with trips geared to a particular interest or hobby. Each of its vessels carries approximately 1,200 passengers and 600 crew. Many of the officers are Dutch and many of the service staff Indonesian but positions are open to all nationalities.

Rotterdam, built in 1959, is considered one of the world's great cruise ships. All the other ships are much newer vessels and two new ships have entered service very recently. A new ship, Veendam, will enter service in 1996.

Ships : *Rotterdam, Noordam, Westerdam, Nieuw Amsterdam, Statendam, Maasdam, Ryndam.*

Cruises : Worldwide, including New York-Caribbean and Alaska (in which it specialises). Rotterdam undertakes an annual world cruise.

Contact : 300 Elliott Avenue West, Seattle. Washington State 98119. USA. Hal Antilles BV, De Ruyterkade 63, PO Box 812, Curaco, Netherlands Antilles.

Employer : Kristina Cruises
Description : A Finnish company offering cruises on the Baltic Sea and Norwegian coast, occasionally further afield. The ships carry 250 and 715 passengers respectively.

Ships : *Kristina Bruhe, Kristina Regina.*

Cruises : Baltic and Norwegian coast.

Contact : Korkeavuorenkatu 2, SF-48100 Kotka. Finland.

Employer : Majesty Cruise Line
Description : Majesty currently operates a single, high-quality cruise ship. It is the upmarket sister company of Dolphin Cruise Line.

Ships : *Royal Majesty.*

Cruises : Specialises in short cruises to the Bahamas and Caribbean from Miami.

Contact : 901 South America Way, Miami. FL33132. USA.

Employer : Marquest
Description : A small-scale cruise line offering adventure cruises but also a high level of service and comfort. Lectures and talks are as frequent as more relaxed entertainments. Carries many German passengers so some knowledge of German would be an advantage.

Ships : *Columbus Caravelle.*

Cruises : North and South America.

Contact : 101 Columbia Street, Suite 150, Laguna Beach. CA92656. USA.

Employer : Mediterranean Cruises
see Epirotiki Line.

Employer : Mediterranean Sun Cruises

Description : A small Greek cruise line operating a single vessel in the Aegean. The vast majority of the crew are Greek.

Ships : *Atalante.*

Cruises : Aegean. Contact : 5 Sachfouri Street, 18536 Piraeus. Athens. Greece.

Employer : Norwegian Cruise Line

Description : NCL operates a fleet of some of the world's largest cruise ships including Norway (1,900 passengers and 800 crew) which was the world's largest until the arrival of Royal Caribbean's Majesty of the Seas. Average number of crew per ship is 700.

With Norwegian officers and an international crew, NCL offers traditional luxury cruising, but at a modest price. NCL's latest ship, Windward, has recently been introduced and carries 1,246 passengers. NCL is one of the Kloster Cruises companies (see Royal Cruise Line and Royal Viking).

Ships : *Dreamward, Norway, Seaward, Southward, Starward, Windward.*

Cruises : Miami, the Bahamas, Caribbean and Mexico, South Pacific, West Coast USA.

Contact : 95 Merrick Way, Coral Gables. FL33134. USA.

Employer : Ocean Cruise Lines

Description : Ocean Cruise Lines is part of the French company Croisieres Pacquet and operates a single ship, currently specialising in offering cruises throughout the Far East. Despite its French origin (would-be crew members should be able to speak French) this line sells its cruises extensively to British passengers.

Ships : *The Pearl.*

Cruises : Far East.

Contact :

Shops and Entertainment Staff: 5 Boulevard Malesherbes, 75008 Paris. France. All Other Positions: Navigestion (Agency) Le Schuylkil, 19 Boulevard de Suisse, Monte Carlo 9800. Monaco.

Employer : Orient Lines

Description : Orient is a fairly new cruise line which offers cruises to more unusual destinations worldwide (Antarctica and the Far East are favourites). The Marco Polo is a fully refurbished ex-Russian ship which can accommodate 800 passengers.

Ships : *Marco Polo.*

Cruises : Worldwide, especially Far East, Antarctica, South Pacific.

Contact : 1510 SE 17th St., Fort Lauderdale. FL33316. USA.

Employer : Paradise Cruises

Description : Operates a single ship from its Cyprus base. Mainly Cypriot crew.

Ships : *Romantica.*

Cruises : Mediterranean only.

Contact : Box 157, Limassol, Cyprus.

Employer : Pearl Cruises

See Ocean Cruise Lines.

Employer : P&O Cruises

Description : P&O is one of the most well known names in the cruise business and their ships carry the P&O name worldwide. P&O ships have high standards and offer traditional, British cruising. The company is undergoing expansion at the moment. It has just introduced its new superliner, *Oriana*, and a massive new ship is under construction for introduction in 1997 (currently codenamed 5956!).

Canberra (1,641 passengers), *Sea Princess* (714 passengers) and *Oriana* (1,760 passengers) have a high proportion of British crew (2,100 in total), although traditionally they recruit many Indian Stewards. Being such a well known company, competition for vacancies is fierce.

Princess Cruises (see this directory) is part of P&O and much larger than its parent. P&O Ferries is a separate division.

Ships : *Canberra, Sea Princess, Oriana.*

Cruises : P&O ships cruise a hectic schedule and visit every corner of the world, including regular round the world cruises.

Contact : Richmond House, Terminus Terrace, Southampton. Hants SO14 3PN

Also : 10100 Santa Monica Boulevard, Los Angeles. CA90067-4189. USA.

Employer : Premier Cruises

Description : Premier is the official cruise line of Walt Disney World and as such attracts a large number of families with children. It provides particularly good entertainment facilities and an informal, relaxed atmosphere on board. It sails out of Port Everglades and Port Canaveral in Florida.

Ships : *Starship Oceanic, Starship Majestic, Starship Atlantic.*

Cruises : 3-4 day cruises, mainly Florida-Bahamas.

Contact : PO Box 517, Cape Canaveral, FL32920. USA.

Employer : Princess Cruises

Description : Princess Cruises is part of the British P&O company, but operates mostly from the USA. It is popular with US cruise passengers although fly-cruise packages are also sold extensively in the UK. Princess Cruises offers luxury cruising, but at a competitive price.

Princess Cruises' ships are some of the newest and most impressive afloat and a brand new ship, Sun Princess, is being introduced this season. Each carries approximately 1,500 passengers (*Sun Princess* 1,950). In the past the company's ships were used to make the steamy TV soap opera 'The Love Boat'!

Employs over 4,500 people, recruited internationally.

Ships : *Crown Princess, Fair Princess, Golden Princess, Island Princess, Pacific Princess, Regal Princess, Royal Princess, Sky Princess, Star Princess, Sun Princess.*

Cruises : Mostly Caribbean, but also further afield including South America, West Coast USA, Hawaii, Europe.

Contact: 10100 Santa Monica Boulevard, Los Angeles. CA 90067-4189. USA.

Also : Richmond House, Terminus Terrace, Southampton. Hants SO14 3PN

Employer : Regal Cruises

Description : Operates a single but very large vessel in the American market. 1,160 passengers can be accommodated.

Ships : *Regal Empress.*

Cruises : Caribbean.

Contact : 4199 34th St. S., Suite B103, St.Petersburg. FL33711. USA.

Employer : Regency Cruise Line

Description : Regency was formed in 1984 and has expanded fast, refurbishing ex-ocean liners for use in the cruise market. The ships offer good standards of accommodation but at a modest price and so attract many first-time cruise passengers.

Ships : *Regent Sun, Regent Sea, Regent Rainbow, Regent Star, Regent Jewel, Regent Spirit.*

Cruises : Caribbean, Alaska, Hawaii, occasionally Mediterranean.

Contact : 260 Madison Avenue, New York. NY10016. USA.

Employer : Renaissance Cruises

Description : Renaissance operates small-scale cruise ships and specialises in cruises for the culturally-minded. Noisy entertainment is rare; lectures and talks are a feature of most cruises. The company's ships are registered in Italy and many crew are Italian.

Ships : *Renaissance I, Renaissance II, Renaissance III, Renaissance IV, Renaissance V, Renaissance VI, Renaissance VII, Renaissance VIII.*

Cruises : Caribbean, Bahamas, Mediterranean and worldwide.

Contact : Suite 300, 1800 Eller Drive, PO Box 350307, Fort Lauderdale. FL33335-0307. USA.

Employer : Royal Caribbean Cruise Line

Description : RCCL is Norwegian owned and one of the biggest cruise lines in the business. Their ships can be identified by the Viking Crown Lounge mounted high up around the funnel. Although traditionally operating in the Caribbean, it now cruises worldwide. At least two ships (usually *Sun Viking* and *Song of Norway*) now cruise the Mediterranean and northern European waters in the summer.

RCCL ships are large and very busy, offering very good service but less space per passenger than most other companies. They have a 'smart but fun' image. The ships carry, on average, 1,000 passengers. The company's marvellous flagship, Majesty of the Seas, can carry 2,354 passengers - making it the biggest cruise ship presently in service in the world and, literally, a floating resort. It is currently based in Miami and cruises the western Caribbean, where it has proved very popular with passengers and crew.

All nationalities are recruited to the crew. Generally, RCCL has fewer crew per passengers than many other lines.

Four new ships (capacity 1,800-2,000 passengers each) are under construction for delivery over the next two years.

Ships : *Sovereign of the Seas, Song of Norway, Song of America, Nordic Empress, Monarch of the Seas, Sun Viking, Viking Serenade, Majesty of the Seas.*

Cruises : Worldwide, mainly Caribbean, Bahamas, Mexico, Mediterranean, northern Europe, including Norwegian fjords, Alaska.

Contact : 1050 Caribbean Way, Miami. FL33132. USA.

Storgaten 26, PO Box 9060, Vaterland. N-0134 Oslo 1.

UK Representation (not Personnel): Inforum House, Addlestone Road, Weybridge. Surrey KT15 2UE

Employer : Royal Cruise Line
Description : As a Kloster Cruises company Royal operates some of the most luxurious ships sailing in the Mediterranean and Aegean. It sells its cruising package holidays mostly in the US and has a higher than average crew-passenger ratio. Many of the crew are Greek. Its operations are now very closely linked with NCL and Royal Viking (below).

Ships : *Star Odyssey, Crown Odyssey, Royal Odyssey.*

Cruises : Mediterranean/Aegean, Caribbean, West Coast USA, Hawaii.

Contact : 1 Maritime Plaza, Suite 1440, San Francisco. CA94111. USA

Employer : Royal European
See Epirotiki Lines.

Employer : Royal Viking Line
Description : Royal Viking operates luxurious ships (500-800 passengers each) sailing both in the Mediterranean and Caribbean and offering luxury cruising. As another Kloster Cruises company, being Norwegian owned, it favours Norwegian officers and European crew. Operations are closely connected with those of NCL and Royal Cruise Line (above).

RVL exceeds the usual 1:2 crew-passenger ratio. So, for example, Royal Viking Sun usually carries 450 crew to serve 760 passengers.

Ships : *Royal Viking Sun, Royal Viking Queen.*

Cruises : Mediterranean, Caribbean.

Contact : 95 Merrick Way, Coral Gables, FL33134. USA. PO Box 100, N-0309 Oslo 3. Norway.

Employer : Sea Escape Cruises
Description : A Scandinavian owned and operated company (international crew) serving the US market. Specialises in one day fun cruises to the Bahamas.

Ships : *Scandinavian Dawn.*

Cruises : Bahamas.

Contact : 8751 W. Broward Boulevard, Plantation. FL33324. USA.

Employer : Seabourn Cruise Line
Description : As a smaller company, Seabourn serves some of the more 'off the beaten track' destinations with two ships (capacity 212 passengers each). It is another Norwegian run company which tends to favour European crew. It specialises in extremely high quality (and very expensive) cruising.

Ships : *Seabourn Pride, Seabourn Spirit.*

Cruises : Mediterranean, South America, Caribbean, South East Asia.

Contact : Strandveien 5C, N-1234 Lysaker. Norway.

55 Francisco Street, San Francisco. CA94133. USA.

Employer : Seawind Cruise Line

Description : Seawind operates from the port of Aruba in the Netherlands Antilles and cruises the south Caribbean (unlike most ships which cruise the north). It attracts many South American passengers and some knowledge of Spanish or Portuguese is an advantage although English is the first language on board.

Ships : *Seawind Crown.*

Cruises : South Caribbean.

Contact : 1750 Coral Way, Miami. FL33145. USA.

Employer : Seven Seas Cruise Line

Description : Japan's only cruise line! Limited potential for non-Japanese crew although the line attracts a number of European travellers.

Ships : *Song of Flower* (265 passengers).

Cruises : South Pacific, occasionally Europe.

Contact : 2-9 Nishi-Shinbashi 1 Chome, Minato-Ku. Tokyo.

Employer : Silversea Cruises

Description : A brand new cruise line operating two super-luxury ships (300 passengers each).

Ships : *Silver Cloud, Silver Wind.*

Cruises : Caribbean, East Coast USA, Europe, Africa.

Contact : 110 E. Broward Boulevard, Fort Lauderdale. FL33301. USA.

Employer : Special Expeditions

Description : Special Expeditions is a small cruise line which specialises in adventure cruises rather than mainstream cruises. Their ships mostly visit small Alaskan and Caribbean ports which are not accessible to large liners. *Sea Cloud* is a sailing yacht.

Ships : *Polaris, Sea Bird, Sea Lion, Sea Cloud.*

Cruises : Caribbean, Alaska.

Contact : 720 5th Avenue, New York. NY10019. USA.

Employer : Star Clippers

Description : Operates very large sail-yachts (180 passengers each) offering 'laid back luxury'. Crew are recruited internationally.

Ships : *Star Clipper, Star Flyer.*

Cruises : Star Clipper in Caribbean year round. Star Flyer spends winters in Caribbean, summers in Mediterranean.

Contact : 4010 Salzedo Avenue, Coral Gables. FL33146. USA.

Employer : Stena Group

Description : This large Swedish based ferry company operates a range of European ferry services but also operates a single cruise liner, capacity 984 passengers.

Ships : *Vancouver Island Princess.*

Cruises : Varies.

Contact : PO Box 31300, S-40519 Gothenburg. Sweden.

Employer : Sun Line Cruises

Description : Sun Line is a Greek owned and operated company operating two small ships and one large ship (Stella Solaris, 640 passengers, 320 crew). It mostly carries US passengers with a majority of Greek crew members. Other English speakers may be accepted.

Ships : *Stella Oceanis, Stella Maris II, Stella Solaris.*

Cruises : Aegean, Mediterranean in summer, Caribbean in winter. Also Amazon River cruises.

Contact : 3 Lassonos Street, 18537 Piraeus. Greece.

Suite 315, One Rockefeller Plaza, New York. NY10020. USA.

Employer : Starlauro
Description : Starlauro has been devastated by the sinking of its much admired 1940's liner *Achille Lauro* in the Indian Ocean in 1994. It is likely that the ship will be replaced (initially by a leased vessel) in due course. Watch this space!

Ships : *Fridtjof Nansen* (568 passengers).

Cruises : Worldwide.

Contact : Piazza del Martiri, 80121 Naples. Italy.

Employer : St. Lawrence Cruise Line
Description : A specialist company operating two small ships and offering cruises on Canada's St. Lawrence River and Gulf.

Note : Employs mostly Canadian nationals.

Ships : *Canadian Empress, Victorian Empress.*

Cruises : Inland/Coastal.

Contact : 253 Ontario Street, Kingston, Ontario. K7L 2Z4. Canada.

Employer : Trans World Cruises
Description : Operates a single vessel from its Panama base.

Ships : *Vasco de Gama.*

Cruises : Caribbean.

Contact : Panama City, Panama.

Employer : Tropical Cruise Line
Description : Operates a single vessel from its Panama base.

Ships : *Southern Elegance.*

Cruises : Caribbean, especially Mexican coast.

Contact : Panama City, Panama.

Employer : Windstar Sail Cruises
Description : Windstar is one of the few companies operating sail cruise ships, each with four sail-carrying masts and auxiliary engine power. Each ship carries 150 passengers and is luxurious but on a smaller scale than the usual cruise ship. Offers high standards but a more relaxed cruising atmosphere. In the current season *Wind Spirit* and *Wind Star* are based in Barbados and *Wind Song* in Tahiti.

Ships : *Wind Song, Wind Spirit, Wind Star.*

Cruises : Caribbean and South Pacific.

Contact : 300 Elliott Avenue West, Seattle, Washington State 98119. USA.

Employer : World Explorer Cruises
Description : World Explorer offers shipboard study courses for students for much of the year. Traditional cruises are offered in the remaining time.

Ships : *Universe.*

Cruises : Various, especially Alaska in summer.

Contact : 555 Montgomery Street, San Francisco. CA94111. USA.

Note : Most of the US cruise lines are fairly small in cruise-ship terms. They are nearly all registered under 'flags of convenience' e.g.. Panama. The only two US-registered ships are operated by American Hawaii.

Carnival Cruise Line is the largest US cruise line by far - all of their ships are Panama/Liberia registered etc.

Note:

Most of the big US cruise lines such as United States Lines went out of business in the 1960's/70's partly due to stringent regulations for US registry, i.e.. must employ all US crew etc. Hence the reason for registering under flags of convenience nowadays, and thereby legally overcoming the regulations.

The biggest cruise lines serving the American market are foreign owned (mostly British or Norwegian) but to all intents and purposes are US cruise lines because their ships rarely cruise anywhere else!

ACCURACY! 'CREWS FOR CRUISE' has the most accurate listing of potential employers you can obtain. All the companies, ships and contacts given here are checked as accurate at time of writing. However, please remember that the industry is developing fast. Cruise lines may open up, close down, move, buy new ships or transfer existing ones without notice.

REMEMBER : These employers do not necessarily recruit all the staff who work aboard their ships. See also the Concessionaires/Agencies section in this book. Most lines recruit internationally and many hold recruiting sessions in London.

USA - Postal Codes : CA - California, IL - Illinois, FL - Florida, MO - Missouri, NJ - New Jersey, NY - New York, RI - Rhode Island, TX - Texas, WA - Washington State.

CHECKLIST

INDEX OF CRUISE LINES

Company :

Date Application Made/
Responses Received/Comments etc. :

Abercrombie & Kent
Airtours
American Canadian Caribbean Line
American Hawaii

Carnival Cruise Lines
Chandris Cruises
Classical Cruise Line
Clipper Cruise Line
Club Med.
Color Line
Commodore Cruise Line
Croisieres Pacquet
Costa Cruises
Crystal Cruises
CTC Cruise Lines
Cunard Line

DFDS
Diamond Cruise
Discovery Cruises
Dolphin Cruise Line

Epirotiki Lines

Hapag Lloyd
Holland America Line

Kristina Cruises

Majesty Cruise Line
Marquest
Mediterranean Cruises

Norwegian Cruise Line

Ocean Cruise Lines
Orient Lines

Paradise Cruises
P&O Cruises
Premier Cruises
Princess Cruises

Regal Cruises
Regency Cruise Line
Renaissance Cruises
Royal Caribbean Cruise Line
Royal Cruise Line
Royal European
Royal Viking Line

Sea Escape Cruises
Seabourn Cruise Line
Seawind Cruise Line
Seven Seas Cruise Line
Silversea Cruises
Special Expeditions
Star Clippers
Starlauro
Stena Group
Sun Line Cruises
St. Lawrence Cruise Line

Trans World Cruises
Tropical Cruise Line

Windstar Sail Cruises
World Explorer Cruises

Notes:

Chapter 8

CONCESSIONAIRES/AGENCIES

Concessionaire/Agency : Allders International
Description : Operates duty free and gift shops on board numerous ships.

Employs/Places : Experienced retail staff.

For (includes) : Holland America Line, Cunard Line, P&O, Princess Cruises.

Contact : 84-98 Southampton Road, Eastleigh. Hants S05 5ZF 1510 SE 17th Street, Fort Lauderdale. FL33316. USA.

Concessionaire/Agency : Apollo Ship Chandlers
Description : Operates shops and concessionary bar/cafe facilities.

Employs/Places : Shop assistants, bar, catering staff.

For (includes) : Regency Cruises, Dolphin Cruise Line, Chandris Cruises, Discovery Cruises.

Contact : 900 NW 43rd Street, Miami. FL33166. USA.

Concessionaire/Agency : Appleton Associates
Description : Recruitment agency.

Employs/Places : Hotel department staff, chefs.

For (includes) : Various.

Contact : 5 Greenway, London N11 3NS

Concessionaire/Agency : Atlantic Associates
Description: Agency providing casino staff for Miami based cruises.

Employs/Places : Qualified and experienced croupiers and other casino staff.

For (includes) : Holland America Line, Cunard Line, Regency Cruises, Discovery Cruises.

Contact : 990 Northwest 166th Street, Miami. FL33126. USA.

Concessionaire/Agency : **Berkeley Bureau**
Description : Provides casino staff.

Employs/Places : Qualified and experienced croupiers and other casino staff, many but not all of which are on cruise ships.

For (includes) : Commodore Cruise Line.

Contact : 11 Cranmer Road, Hampton Hill. Middx. TW12 1DW

Concessionaire/Agency : **Berkeley Scott Selection**
Description : Recruitment agency.

Employs/Places : Chefs.

For (includes) : P&O.

Contact : 11-13 Ockford Road, Godalming. Surrey GU7 1QU

Concessionaire/Agency : **Casinos Austria International**
Description : Operation of casinos, many but not all of which are on cruise ships.

Employs/Places: Experienced casino staff and croupiers.

For (includes) : Various.

Contact : 35 Dover Street, London W1X 3RA 555 NE 15th Street, Plaza Venetia, Miami. FL33132. USA.

Concessionaire/Agency : **City Fitness**
Description : Provides health and fitness instructors for cruise ships. Small number of appointments each year.

Employs/Places : Qualified health and fitness instructors.

For (includes) : Various.

Contact: Suite 214, Butlers Wharf, Shad Thames, London SE1 2YE

Concessionaire/Agency : Coiffeur Transocean

Description : Operates hair and beauty salons, fitness and massage facilities. Controls around 300 personnel who work on a sub-contract basis.

Employs/Places : Hairdressers, beauty therapists, fitness directors, massage therapists.

For (includes) : Various.

Contact : 4th Floor, Swiss Cottage House, Swiss Terrace, Swiss Cottage, London NW6 4RR

Concessionaire/Agency : Cruise Line Appointments

Description : Employment agency.

Employs/Places : Various.

For (includes) : Various.

Contact : 142 Parkwood Road, Bournemouth BH5 2BW

Concessionaire/Agency : Cruiseship Picture Co. Inc.

Description : Provides photographers for cruise ships and operates photographic concessions.

Employs/Places : Experienced photographers.

For (includes) : Various.

Contact : Suite 200, 1177 South America Way, Miami. Fl33132. USA. also at: 101 High Street, Esher, Surrey KT10 9QE

Concessionaire/Agency : G.L. Productions

Description : Provides entertainers for cruise ships.

Employs/Places : Various, all types of acts considered.

For (includes) : Carnival Cruise Lines.

Contact : 1922 NE 149th Street, New York. NY33181. USA.

Concessionaire/Agency : Greyhound Leisure Services

Description : Operates gift and other cruise ship shops on a concessionary basis.

Employs/Places : Shop assistants and manager/esses.

For (includes) : Chandris Cruises, Royal Caribbean Cruise Line, Costa Cruises, Regency Cruise Line, Commodore Cruise Line.

Contact : 8052 NW 14th Street, Miami. FL33126. USA.

Concessionaire/Agency : Info-Cruise

Description : Offers a range of services including employment agency and recruitment seminars. Based in the Netherlands but used by various nationalities.

Employs/Places : Various.

For (includes) : Various.

Contact : PO Box 23195, 1100DR Amsterdam. Netherlands.

Concessionaire/Agency : International Cruise Shops

Description : Operates a variety of concessionary shops aboard large cruise ships. Mainly Caribbean based.

Employs/Places : Retail associates (managers and assistants).

For (includes) : Various.

Contact : PO Box 592355, Miami. FL33159. USA.

Concessionaire/Agency : Logbridge Ltd.

Description : Provides staff for a number of cruise ships, including the QE2.

Employs/Places : Various including chefs, cooks, waiters/waitresses, bar staff, stewards/stewardesses, wine waiters, cleaning staff and restaurant management.

For (includes) : Mainly Cunard.

Contact : South Western House, Canute Road, Southampton. Hants SO14 3NR

Concessionaire/Agency : Marcello Productions

Description : Provides entertainers for cruise ships.

Employs/Places : Various, all types of acts considered.

For (includes) : Carnival Cruise Lines, Royal Caribbean.

Contact : 230 SW 8th Street, Miami. FL32130. USA.

Concessionaire/Agency : Meyer Davis Agency

Description : Provides musicians for cruise ships.

Employs/Places : All types of musicians considered for placement.

For (includes) : Various.

Contact : West 57th Street, New York. NY10019. USA.

Concessionaire/Agency : MMSL

Description : One of the main mainland European agencies. Provides staff for cruise line companies.

Employs/Places : Various, mainly stewards/stewardesses etc.

For (includes) : Various.

Contact : Kristen 20, A-6094 Axams, Austria.

Concessionaire/Agency : Navigestion

Description : An employment agency which recruits crew for a variety of positions on cruise ships.

Employs/Places : Various jobs are handled, but applicants must usually speak good French.

For (includes) : Croisieres Pacquet, Ocean Cruise Lines.

Contact : Le Schuylkil, 19 Boulevard de Suisse, Monte Carlo 9800. Monaco.

Concessionaire/Agency : Ocean Images

Description : Provides photographers.

Employs/Places : Photographers.

For (includes) : P&O, Princess Cruises.

Contact : 7 Home Farm, Lockerley Hall, Romsey. Hants SO51 0JT

Concessionaire/Agency : Poseidon Services Ltd.
Description : Provides representative and management services for a large number of cruise lines operating out of Miami. May be useful for contacts.

Contact : 1007 North America Way, Miami. FL33132. USA.

Concessionaire/Agency : Premier Dance Productions
Description : Agency providing entertainment staff to hotels and nightclubs. Some but not all vacancies are on board cruise ships.

Employs/Places : Entertainers, various types.

For (includes) : Various.

Contact : 26 Chance Road, Wellingborough. Northants NN8 1NR

Concessionaire/Agency : Princess Boutiques/ Princess Casinos
Description : Operates shops and casinos. Employs/Places : Shop assistants, managers, croupiers.

For (includes) : P&O, Princess Cruises.

Contact : 10100 Santa Monica Boulevard, Los Angeles. CA90067-4189. USA.

Concessionaire/Agency : Quest
Description : Agency.

Employs/Places : Hairdressers, beauticians, massage staff.

For (includes) : P&O, Princess Cruises.

Contact : 57 The Broadway, Stanmore, Middx HA7 4DU

Concessionaire/Agency : Quest Marine Services

Description : Agency providing staff for a variety of cruise ship positions, both to cruise lines and concessionary facilities.

Employs/Places : Head chefs, sous chefs, wine waiters, barmen, stewards and stewardesses, gift shop staff, photographers, children's entertainers, purser's staff, casino staff.

For (includes) : Prestigious cruise lines, including Princess Cruises.

Contact : Binning House, 4-6 High Street, Eastleigh. Hants S06 5LA

Concessionaire/Agency : RG International

Description : Agency providing staff to cruise line companies, amongst other international hotel/leisure facilities.

Employs/Places : Various from time to time, mostly stewards and stewardesses etc.

For (includes) : Various.

Contact : 7 Buckland Road, Maidstone. Kent ME16 OSJ

Concessionaire/Agency : Roger James Music

Description : Provides musicians for cruise ships.

Employs/Places : All types of musicians considered for placement.

For (includes) : Various.

Contact : 45 West Street, Los Angeles, CA90039. USA.

Concessionaire/Agency : Sea Chest Associates

Description : Runs a variety of shops and provides staff to cruise lines.

Employs/Places : Mainly gift shop staff.

For (includes) : Various.

Contact : 7385 West Roadway, New Orleans. USA.

Concessionaire/Agency : Southern Games

Description : Provides casino staff.

Employs/Places : Qualified and experienced croupiers and other casino staff.

For (includes) : Various.

Contact : 202 Fulham Road, London SW10 9NB

Concessionaire/Agency : Steiner Group

Description : Operates hair and beauty salons and fitness facilities on prestigious cruise liners.

Employs/Places : Qualified and experienced hair stylists, beauty therapists and fitness instructors. Once accepted, applicants undergo further training at the Steiner Maritime Academy prior to joining a ship. Around 350 staff at any one time.

For (includes) : Cunard, P&O, Costa Cruises, Holland America, Carnival Cruise Line, Chandris.

Contact : Vicki Schaverien, 57/65 The Broadway, Stanmore. Middx HA7 4DU

Concessionaire/Agency : Suncoast Cruise Services

Description : Operates shipboard shop concessions and provides staff to cruise lines.

Employs/Places : Experienced retail staff.

For (includes) : Carnival Cruise Lines.

Contact : 2335 NW 107th Avenue, Miami. FL33172. USA.

Concessionaire/Agency : Trans Ocean Photo

Description : Provides photographers and operates photographic concessions.

Employs/Places : Experienced photographers.

For (includes) : Various, including Holland America.

Contact : 711 12th Avenue, New York. NY10019. USA.

Concessionaire/Agency : V Ships

Description : Agency.

Employs/Places : Various.

For (includes) : Airtours.

Contact : 'Aigue Marine', 24 Av. de Fontvieille, PO Box 639, MC98013. Monaco.

Concessionaire/Agency : VIP International

Description : Agency providing mainly restaurant and galley staff.

Employs/Places : Various, especially chefs and silver service waiters and waitresses. Also gift shop staff.

For (includes) : Various including Royal Caribbean Cruise Line.

Contact : 17 Charing Cross Road, London WC2H OEP

One final useful contact :

The Hotel and Catering Training Company occasionally have information on current hotel and catering vacancies aboard cruise ships.

They can be contacted at 3 Denmark Road, London WC2.

Notes:

Chapter 9

TELL US YOUR STORY ....

'CREWS FOR CRUISE' interviews three crew members and asks for their opinions on life on board ship!

CASE STORY NUMBER ONE

Name : Michael Griffiths
Age : 23
Home Town : Slough, Berkshire.
Job : Restaurant Steward/Waiter
Cruising in : The Caribbean

"Michael, tell us exactly what your job involves?"

"At the moment, I'm serving and waiting in the main dining room as part of a two-man team. I'm actually the junior part of the team, and much of my work is fetching and carrying, serving starters, and the vegetables."

"What sort of special skills do you need for this job?"

"On this particular ship, silver service knowledge is essential. You couldn't do the job without it."

"What training and experience do you have for this job?"

"Well, first of all, I worked for one year, in a local bistro. Then, I applied for a job in a small four star hotel - they gave me most of my professional training and I gained a great deal of experience which I think held me in good stead when I applied for work on the cruise lines. Finally, I worked for one year in a large Trust House Forte hotel before coming here."

"How did you find out about this job?"

"From an advertisement in 'Overseas Jobs Express', placed by one of the employment agencies. Before that, I'd never even thought of working on a ship."

"How did you apply?"

"Initially, I contacted The Lightning Laser CV Company. They were recommended to me because they offer a CV service that's geared to help finding work on cruise ships. Anyway, they produced a very convincing-looking CV for me and I sent it off with a photograph and references from my previous job. Absolutely nothing happened! Then, after about three months, I had a 'phone call from the agency asking me to come in for an interview. They offered me a job two days later on condition I could start within a week!"

"What sort of contract are you working on?"

"At the moment, It's a six month contract with no guaranteed extension. If it is extended, it's usual to get 12 months next time."

"Would you tell me about your pay, as there are so many myths about exactly how much you can earn on board, and indeed, how much you can save?"

"OK. Our basic pay is US$400 per month. That's about £275 at the moment. However, we obviously count on tips, which are usually very good. In the last three months, I've earned US$1,750, US$1,880 and US$1,940. That's a total of US$5,570, and out of that, I have easily saved $4,000 or just over £2,700. I should easily make over £15,000 and save about £10,000 this year, which I want to put down as a deposit on a house."

"What about your working hours etc.?"

"We work permanent split shifts - 11.15am-2.30pm and 6.30pm-10.30pm every day with a complete day off about once every three weeks. Every week there's a 'best waiter' contest and the winner gets an extra day off in port."

"How about your time off ?"

"The crew facilities are good, with two bars, a gym, video room etc. We can use the ship's pool, health club and cinema at the end of each 12-day cruise - before the new passengers embark. We don't get time off in every port but so far this month I've been ashore at Nassau in the Bahamas, Cancun and Cozumel (Mexico)."

"How would you describe the life on board generally?"

"Well, it's certainly hard work at times and it can be downright hectic! But I really love the life and the camaraderie on board is fantastic. I've already made many friends and the parties in the evenings after work are terrific fun!"

"Would you recommend the life?"

"Providing you're an outgoing, adventurous sort of person and you love to travel, I really don't think there's anything to beat it - but I should say, that it might not appeal to everyone, as I've already said, it can be pretty hard work at times."

"Will you come back again if your contract is renewed?"

"Yes. Definitely yes!"

CASE STORY NUMBER TWO

Name : Jane Wilkinson
Age : 26
Home Town : Manchester
Job : Gift Shop Assistant
Cruising in : Miami - The Bahamas

"Jane, tell us who you work for and what do they pay you?"

"I work for a concessionaire actually and it's an American company. They operate three shops on board this ship - a general store cum pharmacy, a gift shop and a clothes boutique. They pay US$1,750 per month flat plus there's a bonus system of up to 25% if we exceed our sales targets."

"Do you think working for a concessionaire is better than working for a cruise line?"

"Well, I know our guaranteed pay is a lot better than many of the line crew. We also get to use the passenger areas on our time off - which they can't. But there is a feeling of 'us-and-them' and so most of the girls I've made friends with are either in the shops or the hair salon."

"How did you get this job"?

"Initially, I purchased a copy of 'Crews for Cruise' - that set me thinking. Then, I used the advice it gave me and wrote to cruise line companies and concessionaires and sent them my CV. I even used the American 'Yellow Pages' to find addresses

(Editors note: **This showed great initiative - well done!**). I think I wrote about

150 letters and in the end, coincidentally, I received two job offers that both arrived in the same post!"

"What about visas?"

"A lot of American companies won't even consider foreigners because of visa problems. I don't need a visa for this job because the ship is registered in, I think, Panama."

"What job qualifications, training and experience do you have?"

"Well, there's no point telling American employers about British qualifications and training schemes, because they don't understand them - and don't want to know anyway! My previous job was working on the perfume and cosmetics counter of a big department store and I think that was what really got me this job."

"What about your hours of work?"

"The shops are open from 9am in the morning to 11pm at night. We work about 65 hours a week each and as long as they are fully staffed we can arrange the work rotas amongst ourselves. We get time off in most ports because the shops are duty-free and so have to close because of Customs regulations."

"Is all your food and accommodation free?"

"No it isn't because we work for a concessionaire. We get a bill every month from the Purser's office - about US$500 (£340), but our boss covers half of it. They also pay our medical insurance."

"Will you come back again if your contract is renewed?"

"I might, but I'd like to try and get a job on one of the luxury ships. I've heard that the pay is a lot better because the cruises are longer and so the passengers spend more."

CASE STORY NUMBER THREE

Name : Martin Groves
Age : 29
Home Town : Loughton, Essex.
Job : Cabin Steward (Room Service)
Cruising in : Worldwide (currently in the South Pacific)

"Martin, what exactly is your job?"

"I'm a Cabin Steward, but I don't actually have anything to do with cabin cleaning and presentation. Basically, we provide 24 hour room service to about 300 cabins -sorry ... staterooms!"

"How did you get this job?"

"I wish I could say it was all down to your book! In actual fact, it was through a friend of a friend I'm afraid - one who worked for a cruise line company, and he gave me some names. I still had to write or 'phone about 40 companies before I found one with a vacancy."

"What experience do you have?"

"I worked as a waiter in a small private hotel for about two years, then they promoted me to Assistant Manager. It's quite common on the ships for crew to be over-qualified for the job they do. And I actually took a pay cut to get this job but I'm having such a great time that I don't really mind about that too much!"

"What's involved?"

"Mainly taking room service orders, making them up, and delivering them to the cabins. During the day, the orders are made up in the main galley. After midnight we have to prepare the drinks and light snacks ourselves, so you do need some catering skills. We make a point of speaking to as many passengers as possible at the start of each new cruise; I like to make friends with them as much as possible and also, if they don't know we're here, they don't order room service - and then we don't get the tips, so it really does pay to be friendly!"

"What sort of contract are you on?"

"Twelve months. But when new Stewards join us, they only get a three month probationer's contract. In the time I've been here, I'd say that about eight in every ten get asked back."

"What future prospects are there?"

"Everyone on a ship hopes to keep moving to bigger ships, as obviously the pay is usually better. We also get priority if a Chief Cabin Steward vacancy comes up. If not, I could go for a management job in the Purser's Department."

"What advice would you give to those seeking a job on a cruise ship?"

"First of all, it's best if you have experience that's relevant to the job you do on the ship. If you don't have it, get it! For my job, if you hadn't done room service in a hotel, not all lines would consider you. Secondly, apply everywhere - if it floats and carries paying passengers apply to work on it. Quite a few of the crew here have started out with the one-ship lines and then applied to the bigger operators; some people even started out on the cross channel ferries."

"Would you recommend the life?"

"Oh yes, definitely! I've really broadened my horizons in both senses. It can be hard work at times but you don't really notice it as you all muck in together and get on with the job."

"How about the social life on board, is it all work and no play?"

"Of course not! You do get some time off obviously, and I've met so many friends among the crew and the passengers that I can quite honestly say that life on board really has changed me as a person. And I think it has also changed my life too; I've er ... met one very special young lady and I'm seriously thinking of asking her to marry me ... but who knows, maybe I'll meet someone even better on the next trip - life on board is like that!"

Chapter 10

CRUISE SHIP ITINERARIES

Some Typical Itineraries for Cruise Ships

Princess Cruises : *Crown Princess*
Ten Night Cruises to the Bahamas, Mexico and the Caribbean.

Fort Lauderdale, Florida	San Juan, Puerto Rico
St. Maarten	St. Thomas
Princess Cays, Bahamas	Montego Bay, Jamaica
Grand Cayman, Cayman Islands	Cozumel, Mexico
Fort Lauderdale	

Cunard Countess
Eight Night Cruises in the eastern Caribbean.

San Juan, Puerto Rico	St. Maarten
Guadeloupe	Grenada
St. Lucia	St. Kitts
San Juan	

Cunard Crown Dynasty
Eleven-16 Night Cruises Including Alaska, US West Coast and the Panama Canal. For Example :

Vancouver	Ketchikan
Tracey Arm Fjord	Skagway
Juneau	Misty Fjord
Victoria	San Francisco
Los Angeles	

Los Angeles	Acapulco, Mexico
Puerto Caldera, Costa Rica	Panama Canal
Cartagena	Ochos Rios, Jamaica
Fort Lauderdale	

Cunard *Vistafjord*
Fourteen Night Cruises in the Canary Islands.

Malaga, Spain	Tangier, Morocco
Lanzarote	Las Palmas
Tenerife	La Palma
Madeira	Gibraltar
Malaga	

Cunard *Crown Monarch*
24 Night Cruises in the South Pacific.

Sydney, Australia	Noumea
Isle of Pines	Tanna
Vila	Honiara
Cairns	Samarai Island
Townsville	Cid Harbour
Whitsunday Islands	Great Barrier Reef
Brisbane	Sydney

Royal Caribbean : *Song of Norway*
Twelve Night Cruises in the eastern Mediterranean.

Barcelona, Spain	Palma, Majorca
Villefranche, France, for Monte Carlo,	Nice, Cannes
Livorno, Italy, for Florence, Pisa	Civitavecchia, Italy, for Rome
Naples, Italy	Messina, Sicily
Corfu, Greece	Venice, Italy

And :

Twelve Night Cruises in the western Mediterranean.

Genoa, Italy	Civitavecchia, Italy, for Rome
Naples, Italy	Katakolon, western Greece
Heraklion, Crete	Rhodes
Patmos	Mykonos
Kusadasi, Turkey	Athens, Greece

Holland America : *Maasdam*
Twelve Night Cruises to Scandinavia and Russia.

Tilbury
Stockholm, Sweden
St. Petersburg, Russia
Copenhagen, Denmark
Tilbury

Kiel, Germany
Helsinki, Finland
Visby, Sweden
Oslo, Norway

P&O : *Canberra*
World Cruise

Southampton
Barbados
Grenada
Panama Canal
Acapulco, Mexico
Honolulu, Hawaii
Auckland, New Zealand
Sydney, Australia
Fremantle, Australia
Kota Kinabalu, Malaysia
Hong Kong
Port Kelang, Malaysia
Colombo, Sri Lanka
Aqaba, Jordan
Haifa, Israel

Madeira
Martinique
La Guaira, Venezuela
Puerto Caldera, Costa Rica
San Francisco
Vava'u, Tonga
Lyttelton, New Zealand
Melbourne, Australia
Bali
Ningbo, China
Singapore
Phuket, Thailand
Bombay, India
Port Said & Suez Canal, Egypt
Athens, Greece
Naples, Italy Southampton

Around the world in 86 days!

Notes:

Kathy M - re: planning application ((call Alice)
Liz - Kate's brother - contact.
- last Camden contact?
email Janelle - re: monies
new Spa near work - enquire re. massage jobs eve
Book flight to Denmark - clare / Jacob
pay gas / electric bill
get roof garden leaflet - work - Iain
email Sirie re: reference

Chapter 11

GLOSSARY OF CRUISE SHIP TERMS
(Plus a few that aren't!!)

Abeam - Off the side of the ship, at a right angle to its length.

Aft - The rear portion of the ship.

Afterdeck - The open area at the aft of the ship.

Alleyway - A small corridor.

Amidships - The centre portion of the ship.

Anchor (At) - Time when the ship is anchored at sea. When a ship is 'at anchor' it is NOT in port.

Astern - At or toward the stern (back) of the ship.

Avast - Behind.

Backwash - Motion in the water caused by the propeller(s) moving in a reverse (astern) direction.

Bar - Sandbar, usually caused by tidal or current conditions near the shore. Or a drink dispensing unit.

Beam - Width of the ship between its two sides at the widest point.

Bearing - Compass direction, expressed in degrees, from the ship to a particular objective or destination.

Below Decks - Any deck below the main deck.

Berth - Dock, pier or quay, also a bed/bunk.

Bilge - Lowest point of the infrastructure in a ship, where bilge water collects.

Bow - The front end of the ship.

Bow Tie - Knot the front end of your neck.

Boat Deck - The deck where the lifeboats or tenders can be accessed.

Bridge - The ship's command and control centre.

Bulkhead - Any wall inside the ship.

Bang head - You probably will.

Bunk - Bed.

Bunk up - Ship board phrase (see 'propeller').

Companionway - Inside passage or stairway.

Course - Direction in which the ship is headed, measured in degrees.

Davit - A device used for raising and lowering the lifeboats.

Dammit - See 'Bang head'.

Deadlight - A ventilated cover to a porthole.

Deck - The floor.

Deckhead - Ceiling.

Dickhead - Idiotic crew member.

Docks - Berths, piers or quays.

Docs - Doctors; handle births, peers and keel-overs.

Draft (or Draught) - Measurement in feet from the ship's waterline to the lowest point of its keel.

Embarkation - The process of loading the ship with new passengers.

Fantail - Rear overhang of a ship.

Fathom - Measurement of distance equal to 6 feet.

Freeport - A port free of Customs regulations or duties.

Funnel - Chimney from which the ship's combustion gasses are propelled into the atmosphere.

Galley - Kitchen.

Gangplank/Gangway - The stairway or jetty by which the ship is entered from the shore.

GRT - Gross Registered Tons/Tonnage. The usual method of measuring the size of passenger ships which relates to the amount of revenue-earning space on board and equal to 100 cubic feet. It is NOT the actual weight of the ship. In fact, this is the standard system of measuring passenger ships used for classification by the Lloyd's Register, the British ship survey and marine insurance society.

Hawser - Rope or cable.

Helm - The apparatus used for steering a ship.

House Flag - The owning company's flag.

Hull - The frame and body of the ship excluding the masts or superstructure.

Inside (Cabin) - A cabin without a window or porthole.

Kedge - A method of moving a ship by means of a hawser attached to an anchor, rarely used nowadays but useful if your ship happens to run aground!

Keel - The underside of a boat/ship.

Keel over - Too much duty-free booze.

Land lubber - A person unfamiliar with the sea.

Leeward - The side which is sheltered from the wind.

Lido - An open deck area, usually for sunbathing, dances etc. and usually having a swimming pool.

Manifest - List of all passengers and crew (and possibly cargo) carried.

Main Deck - The deck which runs the full length of the ship at its longest point.

Muster Stations - Emergency assembly points, used in preparation for boarding the lifeboats.

Outside (Cabin) - A cabin with a window or porthole. Note: If you're offered a choice of cabins, choose one of these!

Pitch - The alternate rise and fall of a ship's bow, which may occur when the ship is under way.

Port - A drink that's always passed to the left hand side of the ship when facing forward at the Captain's table

Porthole - Small round window.

Pothole - Small round hole.

Potty - Small round pot.

Promenade Deck - The deck where it is possible to walk right round the ship on the outside.

Propeller - See 'screw'.

Quay - Berth, dock or pier.

Quack - See 'Docs' or ducks.

Roll - The pendulum-like motion from side to side, which may occur when the ship is under way or you're under the weather.

Rudder - A fin-like device astern and below the waterline, used for steering the vessel.

Screw - The ship's propeller that turns round (not to be confused with 'screwing around' which can also take place on board but means something quite different).

Smokestack - See 'funnel'.

Smokescreen - Too many duty-free cigarettes.

Stabiliser - A computer-controller fin which stabilises the ship in rough seas.

Starboard - Right hand side of the ship when looking forward.

Stern - Rear portion of the ship and the opposite of the bow.

Swell - Unevenness of the sea surface caused by undulating waves usually far apart, that do not break. Also an Americanism meaning terrific.

Tender - A small boat often carried on board ship, used for ship to shore transfers whilst ship is at anchor. Usually stored at the rear of the ship, hence the expression oft' used by the Captain viz "I've got a small tender behind".

Tendering - A procedure by which passengers are transferred to/from the ship by tender. Done where a port is too small for the ship to berth next to the quay, or where there is no port. If there's no port, try brandy.

Topside - The decks above the main deck.

Topless - Not recommended.

Wake - Funereal track of agitated water left behind a ship when in motion.

Waterline - Not to be confused with Bikini-line. The level at which the water reaches on the side of the ship. Also used to refer to decks which are above/ below the waterline.

Windward - The side toward which the wind is blowing (opposite to leeward).

Yaw - Erratic deviation from the ship's set course, usually caused by a heavy sea ... or drunk captain (yaw joking of course).

Yawn - Time for bed.

TEN RULES (AND 'SOD'S LAW') OF WORKING

THE CRUISE SHIPS ....

1. Job offers are like buses. Nothing all week - then three arrive together!

2. Most job offers come between midnight and 6am - when you have been out on the town the night before.

3. If you are offered a choice of crew cabins you will always unknowingly pick the one nearest to the engine room.

4. If you pass your soup ladle or coffee pot over a passenger's head, then the ship WILL hit a freak wave at that moment.

5. The passengers you try hardest to please are the only ones who complain.

6. Your time off ashore always coincides when the ship is berthed in a container port   -never in the Bahamas or Jamaica.

7. But - if you do get a day off in Jamaica that will be the only day it rains for six months.

8. When visiting Mexico you WILL get Montezuma's Revenge.

9. The most talked-about cabin parties only ever take place when you are ON duty.

10. The wealthier the passenger, the less they tip. (Absolutely true)

Questions that passengers (and first-time crew members) have asked !

"Do the crew sleep on board?"

"Is the doctor qualified?"

"What time does the midnight buffet start?"

"Is dinner served in the dining room?"

"Where do we catch the bus for the walking tour?"

"When the ship anchors tomorrow, will we be able to walk ashore?"

"Are the entertainers paid?"

"What time is the four o'clock tour?"

"Will the ship wait for the tour buses to get back?"

"Do we have to stay up until midnight to change our clocks?"

"Will we actually see the equator when we cross it?"

"Will I get wet if I go snorkelling?"

"Will this elevator take me to my cabin?"

"How many fjords to the dollar?"

"Is the mail brought on by ˉplane?"

"Does the ship dock in the middle of town?"

"Who's driving the ship if the Captain's at the cocktail party?"

"Is the island surrounded by water?" "I'm married, but can I come to the Singles Party?"

"Should I put my luggage outside my cabin door before or after I go to sleep?"

"Is the toilet flushed through a hole in the ship's bottom?"

"If I put on weight, will I have to pay extra?"

"Was the fish caught this morning by the crew?"

Overheard on a Greek Island cruise. "Why did the Greeks build so many ruins?"

Overheard in the dining room. "Waiter, this vichyssoise is cold, get me a hot one."

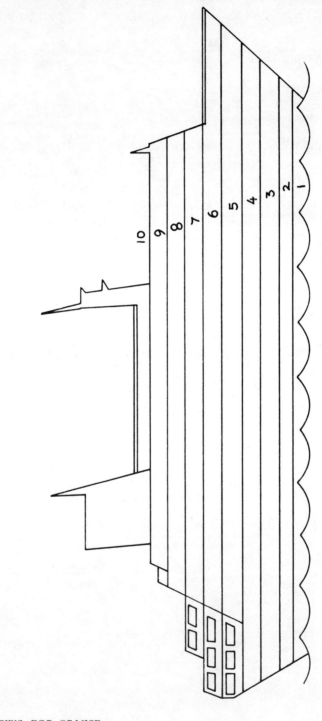

FINDING YOUR WAY AROUND THE SHIP

DECK 10 - The Sun Deck

The sunbathing lido and cocktail lounge.

DECK 9 - The Lido Deck

The poolside lido area. Swimming pools. Jacuzzi. Deck sports. Cafe/ice cream parlour. Poolside bar and barbecue.

DECK 8

Luxury staterooms/suites with verandahs. The ship's casino.

DECK 7

Deluxe staterooms with balconies.

DECK 6 - The Boat Deck

The main restaurant and galley, reception, Purser's office, exchange office, travel agency, duty free shop, gift shops, boutiques, several bars and lounges.

DECK 5 - The Promenade Deck

The cabaret lounge gallery, several lounge bars, the nightclub, library, card and games rooms.

DECK 4

The cabaret lounge dance floor, cinema, photo shop, hair and beauty salon, nursery and children's centre. Superior grade twin cabins.

DECK 3

Standard grade twin cabins, both inside and outside.

DECK 2

Budget grade twin cabins, both inside and outside. The medical centre, health club, part crew accommodation.

DECK 1

Part crew accommodation, the print shop, workshops, various offices.

The Last Word!

Having read this book, it is no good just sitting back to wait for job offers. You do actually have to make a real concerted effort to do something about getting started. Whether you do that now, or put this book in a drawer and say to yourself "I'll do it next week/month/year" is obviously up to you. To be honest, a few people do write to me occasionally and complain that this book didn't work ... to those people I say this. 'Crews for Cruise' does work if you want it to work; and I have hundreds of letters from people who have used the tips and advice in it to gain successful employment on board cruise ships. But ... (and I make no apologies for this) it is certainly not a magic wand! So what will YOU do? Will you get started now - this minute ... or will you open a drawer? Remember, if you open that drawer, you could be waving goodbye to a truly great career filled with fun, excitement and great rewards; I'll leave it to you to decide.

Good Luck!

John Kenning